Getting Started
in Parapsychology

Getting Started
in Parapsychology

Compiled by

Carlos S. Alvarado, Ph.D.

Parapsychology Foundation, Inc.
New York
2002

Published and distributed by
Parapsychology Foundation, Inc.

P. O. Box 1562
New York, NY 10021
Tel: 212-628-1550
Fax: 212-628-1559
http://www.parapsychology.org
Email: info@parapsychology.org

ISBN: 0912328-87-8

❖ Table of Contents

❖ A Brief Overview of English-Language Materials*

Like any other discipline, throughout the years parapsychology has been accumulating literature that is difficult to handle in a short period of time. Consequently, one of the problems that faces beginning students of parapsychology and teachers is where to find information about the field. This bibliographical essay is an attempt to familiarize students and teachers with different sources and with the tools available to search the English-language literature of parapsychology. My purpose is not to present extensive or exhaustive bibliographies, but to be of help in identifying the resources that will lead you to further information about your particular interests. As in any bibliography this one reflects the personal preferences of the compiler. This being the case, readers will find a balance by searching for the topics in which they are interested using the resources listed here. Another word of caution: I have not included critical comments about the sources I have listed. Although I think all of them are useful, many certainly contain mistakes or omissions that diminish their value. For this reason it is important to read with a critical sense, to use different sources, and to go to the primary literature as often as possible.

---

* This is a revised version of an essay published in the *International Journal of Parapsychology* (2000, 11(1), 199-211). The essay is dedicated to Rhea A. White, whose important contributions to parapsychological bibliography have inspired me over the years.

First Contact

Probably the best and most current textbook for classroom use is the third edition of Harvey J. Irwin's *Introduction to Parapsychology* (3rd ed., Jefferson, NC: McFarland, 1999). Other comprehensive textbooks are:

> Edge, H., Morris, R. L., Palmer, J. & Rush, J. (1986). *Foundations of Parapsychology: Exploring the Boundaries of Human Capability.* Boston, MA: Routledge & Kegan Paul.
>
> Nash, C. (1986). *Parapsychology: The Science of Psiology.* Springfield, IL: Charles C Thomas.
>
> Stokes, D.M. (1997). *The Nature of Mind: Parapsychology and the Role of Consciousness in the Physical World.* Jefferson, NC: McFarland.

Another useful overview is John Beloff's *Parapsychology: A Concise History* (London: Athlone Press, 1993). Beloff discusses the topics of preference in parapsychology at different time periods. Readers interested in the history of parapsychology should consult more detailed studies such as the following:

> Crabtree, A. (1994). *From Mesmer to Freud: Magnetic Sleep and the Roots of Psychological Healing.* New Haven, CT: Yale University Press.
>
> Gauld, A. (1968). *The Founders of Psychical Research.* London: Routledge & Kegan Paul.
>
> Inglis, B. (1977). *Natural and Supernatural: A History of the Paranormal from Earliest Times to 1914.* London: Hodder and Stoughton.

Inglis, B. (1984). *Science and Parascience: A History of the Paranormal, 1914-1939.* London: Hodder and Stoughton.

Mauskopf, S.H., & McVaugh, M.R. (1980). *The Elusive Science: Origins of Experimental Psychical Research.* Baltimore: Johns Hopkins University Press.

Moore, R.L. (1977). *In Search of White Crows: Spiritualism, Parapsychology, and American Culture.* New York: Oxford University Press.

Oppenheim, J. (1985). *The Other World: Spiritualism and Psychical Research in England, 1850-1914.* New York: Cambridge University Press.

Additional reviews of the field include those written for the general public. Some of these include:

Broughton, R.S. (1991). *Parapsychology: The Controversial Science.* New York: Ballantine Books.

Eysenck, H.J., & Sargent, C. (1993). *Explaining the Unexplained: Mysteries of the Paranormal.* London: Prion.

Mishlove, J. (1993). *The Roots of Consciousness: The Classic Encyclopedia of Consciousness Studies.* Tulsa, OK: Council Oaks.

Radin, D. (1997). *The Conscious Universe: The Scientific Truth of Psychic Phenomena.* San Francisco: Harper-Edge.

Radin's book is limited to a large extent to experimental work in the field. An interesting and novel overview for the general public is the CD-Rom encyclopedia *Psi Explorer* developed by Mario Varvoglis (for information see http://www.psiexplorer.com). This is not limited to information about phenomena or research, but it is rich in illustrations and bibliography. It also has built-in experiments for the reader's entertainment.

I would also recommend other older popular books that, while not current, are good general introductions to parapsychology up to the date of publication. These are:

Bowles, N., & Hynds, F. with Maxwell, J. (1978). *Psi Search*. New York: Harper & Row.

Douglas, A. (1977). *Extra-sensory Power: A Century of Psychical Research.* Woodstock, NY: Overlook Press.

Hintze, N., & Pratt, J.G. (1975). *The Psychic Realm: What Can You Believe?* New York: Random House.

Inglis, B. (1985). *The Paranormal: An Encyclopedia of Psychic Phenomena.* London: Granada.

Rogo, D.S. (1975). *Parapsychology: A Century of Inquiry.* New York: Taplinger.

In *A Brief Manual for Work in Parapsychology* (New York: Parapsychology Foundation, 1999), there are many useful introductory discussions about methodology from the point of view of conducting research. This includes discussions about controls in experimental research, survey research, meta-analysis, and other issues.

The pre-1930 literature, and the European scene, are discussed in René Sudre's *Parapsychology* (New York: Citadel Press, 1960; first published in French in 1956). But those interested in this literature should start their study by reading some of the older survey books. This list includes such works as:

Barrett, W.F. (1911). *Psychical Research.* London: Williams & Norgate.

Carrington, H. (1930). *The Story of Psychic Science.* London: Rider.

Holms, A.C. (1969). *The Facts of Psychic Science and Philosophy Collated and Discussed.* New Hyde Park, NY: University Books. (First published in 1925).

Richet, C. (1975). *Thirty Years of Psychical Research.* New York: Arno Press. (First published in French in 1922).

David C. Knight's *The ESP Reader* (New York: Grosset & Dunlap, 1969) provides many excerpts of writings related to mediums and to well-known cases of the past.

In addition, the beginning student should be aware of the skeptical literature. This includes:

Alcock, J. (1981). *Parapsychology: Science or Magic?* Elmsford, NY: Pergamon Press.

Alcock, J. (1990). *Science and Supernature: A Critical Appraisal of Parapsychology.* Buffalo, NY: Prometheus.

Frazier, K. (1998). *Encounters with the Paranormal.* Amherst, NY: Prometheus Books.

Hansel, C.E.M. (1989). *The Search for Psychic Power: ESP and Parapsychology Revisited.* Buffalo, NY: Prometheus Books.

Hines, T. (1988). *Pseudoscience and the Paranormal: A Critical Examination of the Evidence.* Buffalo, NY: Prometheus Books.

Hyman, R. (1989). *The Elusive Quarry: A Scientific Appraisal of Psychical Research.* Buffalo, NY: Prometheus Books.

Kurtz, P. (Ed.) (1985). *A Skeptic's Handbook of Parapsychology.* Buffalo, NY: Prometheus Books.

Neher, A. (1990). *Paranormal and Transcendental Experience.* Mineola, NY: Dover.

Zusne, L., & Jones, W.H. (1989). *Anomalistic Psychology: A Study of Magical Thinking* (2nd. ed.). Hillside, NJ: Lawrence Erlbaum Associates.

Other books that review specific areas and phenomena of the field are listed on Table 1.

Additional books not mentioned in the text appear in Appendix A.

There are many places to obtain these books. You may order books in print and out of print from such well known on-line bookstores as Amazon (http://www.amazon.com), and Barnes and Noble (http://www.bn.com). These websites are also good places to search for recent books you may have missed. Searches may be conducted using such key terms as "parapsychology," "psychical research," "paranormal," "psychic phenomena," or "ESP," among others. You may also check *Books in Print*, a standard source available in many American college libraries that has a CD-Rom version. This multi-volume work can be searched by author, title, and by Library of Congress subject headings. For out of print books I recommend *BookFinder.com* (http://www.bookfinder.com), a search engine that connects with several book services that either carry used books themselves, or display the holdings of small used bookstores throughout the United States and in some European countries. There are, of course, many other options on the web such as:

Abebooks (http://www.abebooks.com)
Alibris (http://www.alibris.com)
Bibliophile net (http://www.bibliophile.net)
ILAB-LILA (International League of Antiquarian Booksellers; http://www.ilab-lila.com)

Table 1
Book-Length Reviews of Specific Areas and Phenomena

Poltergeists	Gauld, A., & Cornell, A. D. (1979). *Poltergeists*. London: Routledge & Kegan Paul.
Altered States and Psi	Kelly, E. F., & Locke, R. G. (1981). *Altered States of Consciousness and Psi*. (Parapsychological Monographs, No.18). New York: Parapsychology Foundation.
Psychokinesis	Robinson, D. (1981). *To Stretch a Plank*. Chicago, IL: Nelson-Hall.
Survival of Death	Gauld, A. (1982). *Mediumship and Survival*. London: Heinemann.
Apparitions and Hauntings	Mackenzie, A. (1982). *Hauntings and Apparitions*. London: Heinemann.
Phenomena in Religious Contexts	Rogo, D. S. (1982). *Miracles*. New York: Dial Press.
Precognition	Zohar, D. (1982). *Through the Time Barrier*. London: Heinemann.
Psi Development	Mishlove, J. (1983). *Psi Development Systems*. Jefferson, NC: McFarland.
Out-of-Body Experiences	Irwin, H. J. (1985). *Flight of Mind*. Metuchen, NJ: Scarecrow Press.
Reincarnation	Stevenson, I. (1987). *Children Who Remember Previous Lives*. Charlottesville, VA: University Press of Virginia.
Psychology and Parapsychology	Schmeidler, G. R. (1987). *Parapsychology and Psychology*. Jefferson, NC: McFarland.
Near-Death Experiences	Blackmore, S. J. (1993) *Dying to live*. Buffalo, NY: Prometheus.
Dream ESP	Ullman, M., Krippner, S., with Vaughan, A. (1989). *Dream Telepathy*. Jefferson, NC: McFarland.
Channeling	Hastings, A. (1991). *With the Tongues of Men and Angels*. Fort Worth: Holt, Rinehart & Winston.
Psychics and Crime-Solving	Lyons, A., & Truzzi, M. (1991). *The Blue Sense*. New York: Mysterious Press.
Healing and PK over Biological Matter	Benor, D. *Healing Research*. (2 vols.) Munich: Helix, 1993-1994
Testing of Psychics	Wiseman, R., & Morris, R. L. (1995). *Guidelines for Testing Psychic Claimants*. Hatfield: University of Hertfordshire Press.
ESP of the Past	Mackenzie, A. (1997). *Adventures in Time*. London: Athlone Press.
After-death communications	LaGrand, L.E. (1999). *Messages and miracles*. St. Paul. MN: Llewellyn.

Other good places for "first contact" with the literature of the field are the different information pages on the Web that present bibliography as well as links to many organizations and researchers in the field. Four of the best places to start are:

Daniels, M. "Psychic Science: Explore Parapsychology"
  (http://www.mdani.demon.co.uk/para/parapsy.htm)
Frasca, S. "Parapsychology Resources on the Internet"
  (http://www.roma1.infn.it/rog/group/frasca/b/parap.html)
Parapsychology Foundation, Inc.
  (http://www.parapsychology.org; check "Psi Info")
Steinkamp, F. "Parapsychology Sources on the Internet."
  (http://www.ed.ac.uk/~ejua35/parapsy.htm)

Also useful, is Dean Radin's (compiler) "Frequently-Asked Questions" [about parapsychology] (http://www.psiresearch.org/para1.html), a document prepared in cooperation with several researchers in the field. This document has basic information about many areas of parapsychology and was especially written for those who are starting to study the field.

In addition to the above-mentioned sources of information, those aspiring to be parapsychologists may find much of interest to read about education in this field. The following publications will give you an idea of the issues involved in studying and conducting research in parapsychology. In addition, White has compiled a list of parapsychology theses and dissertations.

Education in Parapsychology. New York: Parapsychology Foundation, 1999.

Palmer, J. "Education in parapsychology" (http://www.rhine.org/PDF%20Files/Education%20in%20Parapsychology.pdf)

Rogo, D.S. (1973). *Methods and Models for Education in Parapsychology* (Parapsychological Monographs No. 14). New York: Parapsychology Foundation.

Shapin, B., & Coly, L. (Eds.) (1976). *Education in Parapsychology.* New York: Parapsychology Foundation.

Smith, M.D. (1999). Educating parapsychologists. *Journal of Parapsychology, 63*, 235-246.

Stanford, R.G. (1978). Education in parapsychology: An overview. *Parapsychology Review, 9*(3), 1-6.

Stanford, R.G. (1984). Parapsychology as a career. *Parapsychology Review, 15*(5), 1-4.

White, R.A. (Comp.) (1996). *Parapsychology Dissertations and Theses: A Multi-Indexed Directory.* New Bern, NC: EHE Network.

For courses and more formal training, check the Summer Study Program of the Rhine Research Center, the courses of the Parapsychology Foundation Lyceum, and the educational opportunities at the Koestler Parapsychology Unit in Scotland. These places are listed in Appendix B.

Bibliographies

Rhea White (http://www.ehe.org) has been active for years in the compilation of bibliographies. Her annotated book-length bibliographies *Parapsychology: Sources of Information* (with Laura A. Dale, Metuchen, NJ: Scarecrow Press, 1973) and *Parapsychology: New Sources of Information, 1973-1989* (Metuchen, NJ: Scarecrow Press, 1990) are the most comprehensive and well-done bibliographies on the subject. The latter presents books under such headings as altered states of consciousness and psi, animal psi, children and psi, criticisms of parapsychology, experimental parapsychology, out-of-body experiences, psychokinesis, religion and parapsychology, spontaneous psi, survival of death, and training and development of psi, among other headings. In addition, the book includes lists of periodicals and organizations as well as a glossary, and several other useful features and essays. White has also produced a variety of shorter but equally useful bibliographies. Some of them are:

White, R. (1988). *Parapsychology for Parents: A Bibliographic Guide.* (2nd ed.). Dix Hills, NY: Parapsychology Sources of Information Center.

White, R. (1989). *Parapsychology for Teachers and Students: A Bibliographic Guide.* Dix Hills, NY: Parapsychology Sources of Information Center.

White, R. (1989). *Parapsychology: Sources on Application and Implications* (2nd ed.). Dix Hills, NY: Parapsychology Sources of Information Center.

White, R. & Anderson, R.I. (1989). *On Being Psychic: A Reading Guide* (2nd ed.). Dix Hills, NY: Parapsychology Sources of Information Center.

White, R. (1989). *Using the Library to Find Out About Parapsychology.* Dix Hills, NY: Parapsychology Sources of Information Center.

White, R. (1990). *Parapsychology: A Reading and Buying Guide to the Best Books in Print* (4th ed.). Dix Hills, NY: Parapsychology Sources of Information Center.

White, R. & Anderson, R.I. (1990). *Psychic Experiences: A Bibliography.* Dix Hills, NY: Parapsychology Sources of Information Center.

White, R. & Anderson, R.I. (1991). *Evidential Bibliography on Psychical Research/Parapsychology.* Dix Hills, NY: Parapsychology Sources of Information Center.

These bibliographies were published by Rhea White's organization Parapsychology Sources of Information Center. In 1990 White created a new organization called the Exceptional Human Experience Network and in 1995 moved to North Carolina. For contact information about this and other organizations see Appendix B.

Other bibliographies of books include Robert Ashby's *Ashby's Guidebook for Study of the Paranormal* (Rev. ed., F. C. Tribbe, Ed., York Beach, ME: Samuel Weiser, 1987) and T. C. Claire's *Occult/Paranormal Bibliography* (Metuchen, NJ: Scarecrow Press, 1984). In addition, see:

McMahon, J.D.S., & Matlock, J.G. (1997). A select bibliography of books on parapsychology, 1991-1994. In S. Krippner (Ed.), *Advances in Parapsychological Research 8* (pp. 277-304). Jefferson, NC: McFarland.

Matlock, J.G., & McMahon, J.D.S. (1994). A select bibliography of books on parapsychology, 1988-1991. In S. Krippner (Ed.), *Advances in Parapsychological Research 7* (pp. 238-271). Jefferson, NC: McFarland.

S. R. Morgan's *Index to Psychic Science* (Swarthmore, PA: Author, 1950) and George Zorab's *Bibliography of Parapsychology* (New York: Parapsychology Foundation, 1957) and "Bibliographie Parapsychologique" (*Les Cahiers de la Tour Saint-Jacques IX* [pp. 103-143]. [Paris]: H. Roudil, n.d., ca 1960) are particularly useful in that they cover the old book and article literature. Zorab's compilations include books and articles published in languages other than English, mainly Dutch, French, German, and Italian.

There are also useful bibliographies on particular phenomena or aspects of parapsychology:

Alvarado, C.S. (Comp.). [Parapsychology Foundation's bibliographies on parapsychological topics] (http://www.parapsychology.org/dynamic/psi.biblio/reading.cfm)
Over 30 1-2 page bibliographies on aspects such as introduction to parapsychology, reference works, education, clinical aspects, development of psychic abilities, survival of death, spontaneous ESP, experimental studies, out-of-body experiences, poltergeists, criticism, and mediumship.

Basford, T.K. (Comp.) (1990). *Near-Death Experiences: An Annotated Bibliography.* New York: Garland.
Berger, J. (Comp.) (1988). Religion and parapsychology: An annotated bibliography of works in the English language. In A. S. Berger and H. O. Thompson (Ed.), *Religion and Parapsychology* (pp. 217-249). Barrytown, NY: Unification Theological Seminary.
Bjorling, J. (Comp.) (1992). *Channeling: A Bibliographic Exploration.* New York: Garland.
Bjorling, J. (Comp.) (1996). *Reincarnation: A Bibliography.* New York: Garland.

Bushman, R. *Bibliographies of the Out-of-Body Experience* (http://www.tower.net.au/~rsb; click on "Bibliographies of the Out-of the Body Experience.")

Crabtree, A. (Comp.) (1988). *Animal Magnetism, Early Hypnotism, and Psychical Research, 1766-1925: An Annotated Bibliography.* White Plains, NY: Kraus International.

Drewes, A., & Drucker, S. (Comps.) (1992). *Parapsychological Research with Children: An Annotated Bibliography.* Metuchen, NJ: Scarecrow Press.

Goss, M. (Comp.) (1979). *Poltergeists: An Annotated Bibliography of Works in English, circa 1880-1975* Metuchen, NJ: Scarecrow Press.

Searching Articles

Journals and Magazines

Although books and on-line documents offer good introductory information about parapsychology, it is important to keep in mind that most of the work that moves the field in terms of research and concepts appears in the form of articles in the journals of the field (for addresses and for titles not mentioned in the text see Appendix C and the links of the Parapsychology Foundation's Website (http://www.parapsychology.org/dynamic/psi.links)

The main articles about parapsychological research and theory are published in:

European Journal of Parapsychology
(http://www.psy.gu.se/ejp.htm)

International Journal of Parapsychology
    (http://www.parapsychology.org/dynamic/
    pubs.ijp)
Journal of Parapsychology
    (http://www.rhine.org/journal.shtml)
Journal of the American Society for Psychical Research
    (http://www.aspr.com/jaspr.htm)
Journal of the Society for Psychical Research
    (http://www.spr.ac.uk/journal.html)

The *Journal of Scientific Exploration* (http://
www.scientificexploration.org/jse.html) also has
important material. However, this journal is not limited to parapsychology, but covers other such areas as
ufology, cryptozoology, and unexplained phenomena belonging to different branches of science. Studying these journals is indispensable for beginning and
advanced students of parapsychology.

There are other valuable publications as well. The
Proceedings of the Society for Psychical Research, published since 1882, appears irregularly. The *Proceedings*
usually contain special monographs, articles, or the
Society's Presidential Addresses. A recently founded
journal covering the whole range of parapsychology
is the *Australian Journal of Parapsychology* (http://
www.aiprinc.org/journal.html). Another informa-
tive publication is *Research in Parapsychology* (RIP).
This is the summary of the proceedings of the annual
conference of the Parapsychological Association
(http://www.parapsych.org), the professional organization of parapsychologists. It contains brief
abstracts of research, theoretical, philosophical,
methodological, and historical papers presented at
the convention in a given year. In addition, *RIP*
includes the full text of the president's address as well
as other invited addresses. *RIP* is particularly useful

as an overview of the recent activities of English-speaking parapsychologists, but it is limited because it consists of abstracts, not full papers. Although *RIP* is behind schedule, issues will continue to appear until they catch up with the 1997 convention. The abstracts have been published in the *Journal of Parapsychology* since 1998. Most of the full papers of these conventions are published for members of the Parapsychological Association (http://www.parapsych.org) and distributed at their annual convention. Although the proceedings can be bought by non-members, they are sold primarily to Parapsychological Association members and only a small number of copies are printed. However, copies of these proceedings can be found in such specialized libraries as the Eileen J. Garrett Library at the Parapsychology Foundation (P. O. Box 1562, New York New York, 10021-0043, USA; http://www.parapsychology.org.dynamic/library.basics), and at the library of the Rhine Research Center (http://www.rhine.org) in Durham, North Carolina. For contact information about the above mentioned institutions see Appendix B.

The *Skeptical Inquirer* (http://csicop.org/si) publishes critiques of parapsychology and articles that offer conventional (e.g., fraud, hallucinations, memory problems) explanations for parapsychological phenomena. Other periodicals focus on the meaning of spontaneous experiences for those who have them (*Exceptional Human Experiences,* http://www.ehe.org/display/ehe-page.cfm?D=74), survival of death, religion, and mystical experiences (*Journal of Religion and Psychical Research*, http://www.lightlink.com/arpr/pub.htm), and near-death experiences (*Journal of Near-Death Experiences,* http://www.iands.org/journal.html). There are, of course, many other publications, such as the numerous popular magazines that cover different aspects of the paranormal. One of these is the *Paranormal Review* (http://moebius.psy.ed.ac.uk/~spr/review.html), a magazine published in London by the Society for Psychical Research.

For a list of other periodical publications (including discontinued ones) see White's *Parapsychology: New Sources of Information, 1973-1989.* (pp. 306-356) mentioned above, and Appendix C.

Indexes, Databases, and Other Resources

In order to find articles and books you need to use a variety of search methods and resources. One of Rhea White's projects has been a paper abstract journal with detailed indexes, *Parapsychology Abstracts International* (PAI), published between 1983-1989. *PAI* contained journal abstracts (and sometimes book abstracts) of parapsychological literature in different languages. *PAI* also contained useful issue indexes and cumulative indexes, features that make this an invaluable reference tool when searching for virtually any subject related to parapsychology. In 1990, *PAI* was reorganized into a journal/abstract periodical called *Exceptional Human Experience* (EHE; http://www.ehe.org/display/ehe-page.cfm?D=74). In its new form, *EHE* is organized under subject headings that refer to specific phenomena (e.g., altered/cognition/perception/states, apparitions, ESP, near-death experiences) and issues (e.g., belief and doubt, science/evidence/pseudoscience, transpersonal psychology). Because the emphasis is now on the variety of anomalous experiences the headings include topics not generally attended to by many parapsychologists such as encounter experiences, kundalini, multiple personality, peak experiences, possession, and religious experience, among others. *EHE* also publishes articles about methodological, conceptual, and transpersonal issues related to parapsychology, with emphases on spontaneous phenomena and examples of a new autobiographical technique that White is developing called "EHE autobiographies" that show how some psychic and other anomalous experiences change lives over a period of time.

In addition, since 1984 White has been compiling a computer database called *PsiLine* "which abstracts and indexes all the major journals from 1940 on, and some for earlier years. It also includes many books from the early twentieth century to date, dissertations, chapters, and conference proceedings" (White, *Parapsychology: New Sources of Information, 1973-1989*, p. 220; see also White, "The Psiline Database System." *Exceptional Human Experience*, 1991, 9, 163-167). This service may be contracted for specific searches for a fee. The system is also available on lease for organizations. For information about searches and leasing, contact Rhea A. White: Exceptional Human Experience Network, 414 Rockledge Road, New Bern, North Carolina, 28562, USA or email her at ehenwhite@cox.net

There are, of course, many other indexes outside of parapsychology useful for finding information about the field. The following are available in some college libraries. The *Psychological Abstracts* is a printed index of abstracts that includes citations to books, and, mainly, abstracts of journal articles. It has a section about parapsychology. *PsychInfo*, an on-line database of journal articles covering different languages, is managed by the American Psychological Association, while its CD-Rom version of English-language materials is *PsychLit*. Other useful electronic indexes include:

Anthropological Literature
Biography Index
Expanded Academic ASAP
International Bibliography of the Social Sciences
Medline
Periodical Contents Index
Social Scisearch
Sociological Abstracts
Religion Indexes
Web of Science

Current Contents presents the table of contents of many journals that may have information about parapsychology or papers on related topics. *Dissertation Abstracts Online* is very useful to locate doctoral dissertations and masters theses. An old and particularly useful resource for the popular literature is the *Reader's Guide to the Periodical Literature*.

J. G. Reed and P. M. Baxter ("Using Reference Databases." In H. Cooper and L. V. Hedges [Eds.], *The Handbook of Research Synthesis* [pp. 57-70]. New York: Russell Sage, 1994) present a useful essay about reference databases. Although not an index, the on-line access to the Library of Congress holdings is very useful for generating lists of books on parapsychological topics (http://catalog.loc.gov).

Literature Reviews

Long articles that review a variety of areas of parapsychology appear in the *Advances in Parapsychological Research* series edited by Stanley Krippner:

> Krippner, S. (Ed.) (1977). *Advances in Parapsychological Research: Vol. 1: Psychokinesis.* New York: Pergamon Press.
>
> Krippner, S. (Ed.) (1978). *Advances in Parapsychological Research: Vol. 2: Extrasensory perception.* New York: Pergamon Press.
>
> Krippner, S. (Ed.) (1982). *Advances in Parapsychological Research 3.* New York: Pergamon Press.
>
> Krippner, S. (Ed.) (1984). *Advances in Parapsychological Research 4.* Jefferson, NC: McFarland.
>
> Krippner, S. (Ed.) (1987). *Advances in Parapsychological Research 5.* Jefferson, NC: McFarland.
>
> Krippner, S. (Ed.) (1990). *Advances in Parapsychological Research 6.* Jefferson, NC: McFarland.
>
> Krippner, S. (Ed.) (1994). *Advances in Parapsychological Research 7.* Jefferson, NC: McFarland.
>
> Krippner, S. (Ed.) (1997). *Advances in Parapsychological Research 8.* Jefferson, NC: McFarland.

Benjamin B. Wolman's *Handbook of Parapsychology* (Jefferson, NC: McFarland, 1986; first published in 1977) is also a valuable collection of comprehensive literature reviews, although the essays are dated and some have been superseded by essays published in *Advances.* A more recent volume with useful articles reviewing different phenomena of parapsychology is the compilation of Etzel Cardeña, Steven Jay Lynn, and Stanley Krippner, *Varieties of Anomalous Experience* (Washington, DC: American Psychological Association, 2000). In addition to review articles about ESP experiences, near-death experiences, out-of-body experiences, healing, and recollections of previous lives, the volume includes discussions of other phenomena such as alien abductions, synesthesia, and hallucinations (http://www.apa.org/books/ 431629A.html).

Other older, but useful sources of survey papers are those books edited by parapsychologists to review different aspects of the field:

Beloff, J. (Ed.) (1974). *New Directions in Parapsychology*. London: Elek.

Grattan-Guinness, I. (Ed.) (1982). *Psychical Research: A Guide to Its History, Principles and Practices*. Wellingborough, Northamptonshire, England: Aquarian Press.

Schmeidler, G.R. (Ed.) (1976). *Parapsychology: Its Relation to Physics, Biology, Psychology and Psychiatry*. Metuchen, NJ: Scarecrow Press.

White, R.A. (Ed.) (1976). *Surveys in Parapsychology: Reviews of the Literature with Updated Bibliographies*. Metuchen, NJ: Scarecrow Press.

K. Ramakrishna Rao has edited two useful volumes. In *The Basic Experiments in Parapsychology* (Jefferson, NC: McFarland, 2001), he has reprinted important experiments of the field. *Case Studies in Parapsychology* (Jefferson, NC: McFarland, 1986), contains papers centering on Louisa E. Rhine's spontaneous case studies. It also includes papers dealing with the spontaneous case work of other researchers on such topics as apparitions, recurrent and non-recurrent physical effects, out-of-body experiences, and reincarnation-type cases.

In addition, the interested reader is referred to the literature review papers which are published occasionally in the above-mentioned parapsychology journals.

Other Reference Works

Perhaps the best glossary in the field is Michael Thalbourne's *Glossary of Terms Used in Parapsychology* (London: Heinemann, 1982). Some terms from the revised edition of this glossary (New York: Puente Publications, 2002) appear in Appendix D. Other useful glossaries are:

> Dale, L., & White, R.A. (1977). Glossary of Terms Found in the Literature of Psychical Research and Parapsychology. In B. B. Wolman (Ed.), *Handbook of Parapsychology* (pp. 921-936). New York: van Nostrand Reinhold.
>
> Grattan-Guinness, I. (1982). A Short Glossary of Terms. In I. Grattan-Guinness (Ed.), *Psychical Research: A Guide to its History Principles and Practices* (pp. 387-399). Wellingborough, Northamptonshire, England: Aquarian Press.
>
> White, R.A. (Comp.) (1990). *Parapsychology: New Sources of Information, 1973-1989.* Metuchen, NJ: Scarecrow Press. (pp. 580-596).

Some encyclopedias have presented definitions of terms, as well as much additional information about parapsychology. An old but still useful one is Nandor Fodor's *Encyclopedia of Psychic Science* (New Hyde Park, NY: University Books, 1969; first published ca. 1933). This work is particularly useful for the student interested in pre-1930 psychical research. More recently, Arthur and Joyce Berger have published their *Encyclopedia of Parapsychology and Psychical Research* (New York: Paragon House, 1991). This work (and Fodor's) include entries about researchers, psychics and mediums, phenomena, journals, organizations, and terms used in the field. Other useful works include:

George, L. (1955). *Alternative Realities: The Paranormal, the Mystic, and the Transcendent in Human Experience.* New York: Facts on File.

Guiley, R.E. (1991). *Harper's Encyclopedia of Mystical and Paranormal Experiences.* San Francisco: Harper San Francisco.

Guiley, R.E. (2000). *The Encyclopedia of Ghosts and Spirits.* (2nd ed.) New York: Checkmark Books.

Melton, J.G. (Ed.) (2001). *Encyclopedia of Occultism & Parapsychology* (5th ed, 2 vols.). Detroit, MI: Gale Research.

Stein, G. (Ed.). (1996). *The Encyclopedia of the Paranormal.* Amherst, NY: Prometheus Books.

Williams, W.F. (Ed.). (2000). *Encyclopedia of Pseudoscience.* New York: Facts on File.

In addition, Brian Inglis's *The Paranormal* (London: Granada, 1985, pp. 300-340) and Helen Pleasants's *Biographical Dictionary of Parapsychology* (New York: Garrett Publications/Helix Press, 1964) present biographical information about psychics, mediums, and researchers.

Concluding Remarks

This short review is by no means exhaustive, but I hope it will be useful as a starting point for the student of parapsychology. Beginning students should keep in mind, however, that books and articles that review aspects of parapsychology are no substitute for studying original reports. Many reviews are short and superficial and do not always cover all aspects of particular studies. Reviewers may focus only on aspects of interest to themselves and miss other aspects of interest to the student. In addition, there are other points to bear in mind when studying the literature of parapsychology. One needs to distinguish between the popular literature, and the more academic and research-oriented literature. Although there is room for all levels and approaches, one must not confuse popular and anecdotal accounts with careful investigations. The popular literature (including the Web) is full of unreliable information, including unsupported claims about psychic development and other issues. Although the academic literature can be too conservative (thus, a little bit boring and "stuffy" for the general reader), one must not forget that there are certain standards to keep to when dealing with topics so uncertain and difficult as those of parapsychology. On the positive side, the popular literature discusses topics ignored by the academic community and is full of valuable experiential material that is a constant reminder of the richness of the phenomena of parapsychology.

We should also keep in mind that when we talk about "the literature" we are not referring only to recent publications. In this bibliographical essay I have emphasized modern publications, but there are many important books and articles published before many of us were born that are still relevant and of basic importance to the field.

I hope the sources cited in this paper will lead the student of parapsychology into this literature and will give him or her an overview of the great number of publications available as well as an indication of the number of hours of study required for acquaintance with the methods, concepts, findings, and theories of this field. Always remember that, regardless of the materials and resources listed in this essay, it is up to you to bring variety, balance, and perspective to your studies in this field.

❖ Appendix A
Additional Bibliography

Almeder, R. (1992). *Death and Personal Survival: The Evidence for Life after Death.* Lanham, MD: Littlefield Adams.
A discussion of the arguments for various aspects of the survival question; namely, reincarnation, out-of-body experiences, apparitions of the dead, and possession.

Auerbach, L. (1986). *ESP, Hauntings and Poltergeists: A Parapsychologist's Handbook.* New York: Warner Books.
A guide for the investigation of spontaneous phenomena, and a brief survey of research that has been done in this area.

Auerbach, L. (1991). *Psychic Dreaming: A Parapsychologist's Handbook.* New York: Warner Books.
A popular work on the relationship of dreams to parapsychological research.

Auerbach, L. (1993). *Reincarnation, Channeling and Possession: A Parapsychologist's Handbook.* New York: Warner Books.
An introduction to phenomena which allegedly "involve the transmigration of a spirit or discarnate entity" (p. 3) including interviews with experts in the field.

Beloff, J. (1990). *The Relentless Question: Reflections on the Paranormal.* Jefferson, NC: McFarland.
Compilation of 16 essays addressing such topics as the nature and credibility of psi, the relationship of parapsychology and science, and the issue of causation.

Braude, S.E. (1986). *The Limits of Influence: Psychokinesis and the Philosophy of Science.* New York: Routledge, Chapman & Hall.
An examination of spontaneous phenomena, arguing for their evidential value in presenting a case for psi.

Carlton, E. (2000). *The Paranormal: Research and the Quest for Meaning.* Burlington, VT: Ashgate.
An overview of parapsychology from the point of view of the different meanings of the phenomena.

Coly, L., & McMahon, J. D. S. (Eds.). (1993). *Psi Research Methodology: A Re-Examination.* New York: Parapsychology Foundation. [Proceedings of 1988 International Conference of the Parapsychology Foundation]
Papers about research methodology in parapsychology, mainly experimental.

Coly, L., & McMahon, J. D. S. (Eds.). (1993). *Psi and Clinical Practice.* New York: Parapsychology Foundation. [Proceedings of 1989 International Conference of the Parapsychology Foundation]
Papers about the mental health implications of psychic phenomena and counseling strategies to help experiencers.

Coly, L., & McMahon, J. D. S. (Eds.). (1995). *Parapsychology and Thanatology.* New York: Parapsychology Foundation. [Proceedings of 1993 International Conference of the Parapsychology Foundation]
Discussions about phenomena suggestive of survival of death such as near-death experiences and reincarnation.

Coly, L., & White, R.A. (Eds). (1994). *Women and Parapsychology.* New York: Parapsychology Foundation. [Proceedings of 1991 International Conference of the Parapsychology Foundation]
Examines the importance of feminist science and the role of women in parapsychology.

Cornell, T. (2002). *Investigating the paranormal.* New York: Helix Press.
Investigation of cases of hauntings, poltergeists and mediums. Chronicles over 50 years of research of the author's career as a psychical researcher.

Doore, G. (Ed.). (1990). *What Survives?: Contemporary Explorations of Life After Death.* Los Angeles: Jeremy Tarcher.
Collection of articles on various aspects of the survival question.

Duncan, L., & Roll, W. (1995). *Psychic Connections: A Journey into the Mysterious World of Psi.* New York: Delacorte.
An overview of parapsychology intended for a young adult audience.

Ehrenwald, J. (1978). *The ESP Experience: A Psychiatric Validation*. New York: Basic Books.
An examination of the relationship between psychiatry and parapsychology focusing on the factors which seem to be conducive to psi.

Felton, D. (1999). *Haunted Greece and Rome: Ghost Stories from Classical Antiquity*. Austin: University of Texas Press.
An examination of tales and beliefs about haunted houses in classical antiquity.

Flew, A. (Ed.). (1978). *Readings in the Philosophical Problems of Parapsychology*. Buffalo, NY: Prometheus.
Collection of 36 articles by noted scholars such as Descartes, Ducasse, Gauld, Murphy, and Rhine.

Garrett, E.J. (2002). *Adventures in the Supernormal*. New York: Helix Press.
Autobiographical account of the experiences, development and opinions of a well-known psychic and medium. Includes reminiscences of Garrett by friends and colleagues in parapsychology and the arts, a brief biography of her life from 1949 to 1970, and a bibliography of works by and about her.

Gauld, A. (1992). *A History of Hypnotism*. New York: Cambridge University Press.
A comprehensive treatment of hypnosis from the eighteenth century to present day applications and theories.

Harpur, P. (1994). *Daimonic reality: A Field Guide to the Otherworld.* New York: Viking Arkana.
An examination of apparitional and visionary experiences (including ghosts, fairies, UFOs, Marian visions, and crop circles), the common threads that tie them together, and the people who have them.

Heaney, J. J. (1984). *The Sacred and the Psychic: Parapsychology and Christian Theology.* Mahwah, NJ: Paulist Press.
Study of the relationship between parapsychology and Christianity, looking at healing, prophecy, and other alleged paranormal powers.

Houran, J., & Lange, R. (Eds.) (2001). *Haunting and Poltergeists: Multidisciplinary Perspectives.* Jefferson, NC: McFarland.
Papers about different aspects and explanations of haunted houses and poltergeist phenomena.

Jahn, R.G., & Dunne, B.J. (1987). *Margins of Reality: The Role of Consciousness in the Physical World.* San Diego, CA: Harcourt Brace Jovanovich.
A survey of the relationship between physics and consciousness and presentation of studies done at the Princeton Engineering Anomalies Research Laboratory.

Kellehear, A. (1996). *Experiences Near Death: Beyond Medicine and Religion.* New York: Oxford University Press.
A unique sociological interpretation of the experiences occurring near death, including deathbed visions and NDEs.

Kelly, E.F., & Locke, R.G. (1981). *Altered States of Consciousness and PSI: An Historical Survey and Research Prospectus.* [Parapsychological Monograph No. 18] New York: Parapsychology Foundation.
A broad perspective of altered states of consciousness research, including anthropological and religious aspects related to psi manifestation and a proposed model for the development of ASC.

McClenon, J. (1984). *Deviant Science: The Case of Parapsychology.* Philadelphia, PA: University of Pennsylvania Press.
A sociological study which surveys parapsychology and its relationship to science in general.

McClenon, J. (1994). *Wondrous Events: Foundations of Religious Beliefs.* Philadelphia: University of Pennsylvania Press.
An experience-centered sociological survey of events that are thought to exceed scientific explanation.

Murphy, M. (1992). *The Future of the Body: Explorations Into the Further Evolution of Human Nature.* Los Angeles: Jeremy Tarcher.
Drawing on medical, psychological, theological, as well as parapsychological sources the author speculates on the future of humankind with emphasis on phenomena of the human body.

Myers, Frederic W. H. (1903). *Human Personality and Its Survival of Bodily Death.* New York: Longmans, Green. 2 volumes. [Later editions were also published including a 1 volume abridged version edited by Susy Smith.]
A model of the role of the subliminal (subconscious) mind in relation to psychopathology, dreaming, creativity, apparitions, telepathy and mediumship. It is argued that all of these phenomena indicate survival of death.

Pilkington, R. (Ed.). (1987). *Men and Women of Parapsychology: Personal Reflections.* Jefferson, NC: McFarland.
Essays and interviews by and about famous figures in parapsychology including Bender, Coly, Ehrenwald, Eisenbud, Schmeidler, Servadio, and Zorab.

Rhine, L.E. (1975). *Psi, What is It? The Story of ESP and PK.* Durham, NC: Parapsychology Press.
A non-technical, introductory survey of paranormal phenomena in the laboratory and in everyday life.

Shapin, B., & Coly, L. (Eds.). (1987). *Parapsychology, Philosophy and Religious Concepts.* [Proceedings of 1985 International Conference of the Parapsychology Foundation]. New York: Parapsychology Foundation.
Papers examining the relevance of psi in religious traditions and philosophical thought.

Shapin, B., & Coly, L. (Eds.). (1989). *Parapsychology and Human Nature.* [Proceedings of 1986 International Conference of the Parapsychology Foundation]. New York: Parapsychology Foundation.
Explorations of psi, including psychokinesis, from disciplines such as psychiatry, psychology, sociology, and anthropology.

Shapin, B., & Coly, L. (Eds.). (1992). *Spontaneous Psi, Depth Psychology and Parapsychology.* [Proceedings of 1987 International Conference of the Parapsychology Foundation]. New York: Parapsychology Foundation.
A discussion of psychological and conceptual aspects of parapsychology with emphasis on spontaneous experiences.

Tyrrell, G. N. M. (1973). *Apparitions.* London: Society for Psychical Research.
An examination of the phenomena of apparitions. The author presents his own model assuming the interaction of human minds through ESP.

Zollschan, G. K., Schumaker, J. F. & Walsh, G. F. (Eds.). (1989). *Exploring the Paranormal: Perspectives on Belief and Experience.* Garden City Park, NY: Avery Publishing.
Interdisciplinary approach to psi by authors such as Braude, Eisenbud, Irwin, and Krippner.

❖ Appendix B
Organizations and Research Centers

Academy of Religion and Psychical Research
http://www.lightlink.com/arpr
PO Box 614, Bloomfield, CT 06002 USA
Phone: 1-860-242-4593
Executive Secretary: Boyce Batey.
Academic affiliate of Spiritual Frontiers Fellowship.
Membership organization. Conferences, library.
Publications: *Journal of the Academy of Religion and Psychical Research*, Proceedings of conferences.

American Society for Psychical Research (ASPR)
http://www.aspr.com/index.html
5 W. 73rd Street, New York, NY 10023 USA
Phone: 1-212-799-5050; Fax: 1-212-396-2497
Executive Director: Patrice Keane.
Membership organization.
Lectures, introductory material, library.
Publications: *Journal of the American Society for Psychical Research, ASPR Newsletter.*

Anomalistic Psychology Research Unit
http://www.goldsmiths.ac.uk/apru
Department of Psychology, Goldsmith College,
University of London, New Cross, London
SE14 6NW England
Director: Prof. Christopher French.
Research on anomalistic psychology.
Publication: *The Skeptic.*

Associazione Italiana Scientifica di Metapsichica

http://www.elemaya.com/Aism/default.htm

Via Pestalozzi 4, 20143 Milan, Italy

email: metapsichica@yahoo.it

President: Dr. Giorgio Cozzi.

Research, lectures, courses.

Publication: *Metapsichica.*

Association for Research and Enlightenment (ARE)

http://www.edgarcayce.org

215 67th Street, Virginia Beach, VA 23451 USA

Toll-free phone in the US: 1-800-333-4499;

Phone: 1-757-428-3588; Fax: 1-757-422-4631

Membership organization.

Conferences, lectures, workshops, library.

Publications: *Venture Inward.*

Australian Institute of Parapsychological Research (AIPR)

http://www.aiprinc.org

PO Box 176, Annandale NSW 2038, Australia

Membership organization.

Meetings.

Publications: *Australian Journal of Parapsychology.*

Centro Studi Parapsicologici

http://digilander.iol.it/cspbologna

Via Valeriani, 39, 40134 Bologna, Italy

Phone & Fax: 39-51-614-3104

email: centrsp@iperbole.bologna.it

President: Dr. Piero Cassoli.

Research, conferences, courses.

Publications: *Quaderni di Parapsicologia.*

Churches' Fellowship for Psychical and Spiritual Studies
http://www.cfpss.freeserve.co.uk
South Road, North Somercotes, Nr. Louth,
Lincolnshire LN11 7PT England
Phone & Fax: 44-1507-358-845
email: gensec@cfpss.freeserve.co.uk
President: Canon Michael Perry.
Membership organization.
Conferences and meetings, study materials.
Publication: *Christian Parapsychologist.*

Cognitive Sciences Laboratory
http://www.lfr.org/csl/index.shtml
330 Cowper Street, Suite 200, Palo Alto, CA
94301 USA
Phone: 1-650-327-2007; Fax: 1-650-322-7960
Executive Director: Dr. Edwin C. May.
Director of Research: James Spottiswoode.
Research, laboratory.

Division of Personality Studies
UVA Health Systems
PO Box 800152, University of Virginia,
Charlottesville, VA 22908 USA
Phone: 1-804-295-9454; Fax: 1-804-924-1712
Director: Dr. Bruce Greyson.
Research on reincarnation cases and near-death
experiences.

Exceptional Human Experience Network
http://www.ehe.org
414 Rockledge Road, New Bern, NC 28562 USA
Phone: 1-919-271-1243; Fax: 1-919-636-8371
Director: Rhea A. White.
Maintains database (PsiLine) with computer search capabilities.
Publications: *Exceptional Human Experience* (formerly *Parapsychology Abstracts International*), *EHE News*, bibliographies on particular topics in parapsychology.

Fondazione Biblioteca Bozzano-De Boni
http://www2.comune.bologna.it/bologna/
fbibbdb/evhmfb.htm
Via Guglielmo Marconi 8, 40122 Bologna, Italy
Phone: 39-51-272-021; Fax: 39-51-554-003
E-mail: fbibbdb@iperbole.bologna.it
Director: Silvio Ravaldini.
Library, conferences, courses, lectures.
Publications: *Luce e Ombra*, books.

Fundação Bial (Bial Foundation)
http://www.bial.pt/int/index.php
A Avenida da Siderurgia Nacional
4745-457 S. Mamede do Coronado
Portugal
Phone: 351-22-986 6100; Fax: 351-22-986-6190
Email: info@bial.com
Director: Dr. Luis Portela.
Research grants, conferences.
Publication: conference proceedings.

Institut für Grenzgebiete der Psychologie und Psychohygiene (IGPP)
http://www.igpp.de
Wilhelmstrasse 3a, D79098
Freiburg im Breisgau, Germany
Phone 49-761-207-210; Fax 49-761-207-2199
Director: Dr. Dieter Vaitl.
Laboratory, field studies, library, grants.
Publication: *Zeitschrift für Parapsychologie und Grenzgebiete der Psychologie* (in German with English summaries.)

Institut Métapsychique International
http://www.imi-paris.org
51 rue de l'Aqueduc, 75010 Paris, France
Phone & Fax: 33-1-4707-2385
Email: imi-paris@Wanadoo.fr
President: Dr. Mario Varvoglis.
Research, library and archives.

Institute of Noetic Sciences (IONS)
http://www.noetic.org
475 Gate Five Road, Suite 300,
PO Box 909, Sausalito, CA 94966-0909 USA
Phone: 1-707-779-7798
Founder: Dr. Edgar D. Mitchell.
President: Winston Franklin
Director of Research: Dr. Marilyn Schlitz.
Membership organization with local groups throughout the country.
Grants, lectures, conferences, travel program.
Publications: *Ions Review.*

Instituto de Psicología Paranormal
http://www.alipsi.com.ar/english.htm
Salta 2015 (1137), Capital Federal,
Buenos Aires, Argentina
Phone: 54-1-305-6724; Fax: 54-11-4305-6724
Email: rapp@fibertel.com.ar
Director: Alejandro Parra.
Research, courses, lectures, library.
Publications: *Revista Argentina de Psicología Paranormal.*

International Association for Near-Death Studies
http://www.iands.org
PO Box 502, East Windsor Hill, CT 06028-0502 USA
Phone: 1-860- 644-5216; Fax 1-860-644-5759
Email: office@iands.org
President: Bill Taylor.
Membership, local support groups
Publication: *Journal of Near-Death Studies, Vital Signs.*

International Society of Life Information Science
http://www.ai-gakkai.or.jp/islis/en/islis.htm
c/o Yamamoto Bio-Emission Laboratory,
National Institute of Radiological Sciences (NIRS),
9-1, Anagawa-4, Inage-ku, Chiba-shi
263-8555, Japan
Phone: 81-53-206-3066; Fax: 81-43-206-3069
Email: islis@nirs.go.jp
President: Dr. Mastoshi Itoh.
Membership, conferences
Publication: *Journal of International Society of Life Information Science.*

International Society for the Study of Subtle Energies and Energy Medicine
http://www.issseem.org
11005 Ralston Rd., #100D, Arvada, CO 80004 USA
Phone: 1-303-425-4625; Fax: 1-303-425-4685
Email: issseem@cs.com
President: Dr. T. M. Srinivasan.
Membership, conferences.
Publications: *Subtle Energies and Energy Medicine, Bridges.*

Inter Psi: Grupo de Estudos de Semiótica, Interconectividade e Consciência
www.interpsi.cjb.net
Centro de Estudos Peirceanos, Programa de Pós-Graduação em Comunicação e Semiótica,
Pontifíca Universidade Católica de São Paulo,
Rua Vicente José de Almeida, 228
Cep 04652-140, São Paulo, Brasil
Email: interpsi@mail.ru.
Coordinators: Fatima Regina Machado and Wellington Zangari.
Research, courses, discussion groups, internet discussion group.
Publication: *Revista Virtual de Pesquisa Psi* (on-line: www.portalpsi.cjb.net)

Koestler Parapsychology Unit (KPU)
http://moebius.psy.ed.ac.uk/gr_index.html
Department of Psychology,
University of Edinburgh
7 George Square, Edinburgh
EH8 9JZ, Scotland
Phone: 44-131-650-3348; Fax: 44-131-650-3369
Professor Robert L. Morris, "Koestler Professor of Parapsychology".
Research, laboratory, Ph.D. program in psychology with thesis in parapsychological topics.

Office of Paranormal Investigations
http://mindreader.com/opi/index.htm
PO Box 875, Orinda, CA 94563 USA
Phone: 1-415-553-2588
Director: Loyd Auerbach.
Staff conducts investigations of purported psi utilizing a team approach.

Österreichische Gesellschaft für Parapsychologie und Grenzbereiche der Wissenschaften (Austrian Society for Parapsychology and Border Areas of Science)
http://parapsychologie.ac.at
Institut für Ethnologie, Kultur und Sozialanthropologie der Universitaet Wien,
A - 1010 Wien,
Universitaetsstrasse 7, Austria
Email: office@parapsychologie.ac.at
Director: Prof. Peter Mulacz.
Lectures, library.

Parapsychological Association, Inc. (PA)
http://www.parapsych.org
P. O. Box 92209, Durham, NC 27708-2209 USA
Phone: 1-919-682-3752; Fax: 1-919-683-4338
Professional international membership organization, member of AAAS.
Disseminates information to the media and public.
Sponsors annual convention. Abstracts of proceedings published in the *Proceedings of the Parapsychological Association* (1957-1971), *Research in Parapsychology* (1972-1997), and in the *Journal of Parapsychology* (1998-forward).

Parapsychology Foundation, Inc. (PF)
http://www.parapsychology.org
P. O Box 1562, New York, NY 10021-0043 USA
Email: info@parapsychology.org
Phone: 1-212-628-1550; Fax: 1-212-628-1559
President: Eileen Coly.
Executive Director: Lisette Coly.
Grants and awards; international conferences;
Eileen J. Garrett Library (for reference only),
PF Lyceum; Perspectives Lectures Series;
PF International Affiliates; Outreach Program;
Psychic Explorers Club.
Publications: *International Journal of Parapsychology*, Proceedings of conferences, *Parapsychological Monographs,* Pamphlet Series, Helix Press.

Princeton Engineering Anomalies Research Laboratory

http://www.princeton.edu/~pear
School of Engineering, C-131 Engineering Quad,
Princeton University, Princeton, NJ 08544 USA
Phone: 1-609-258-5950; Fax: 1-609-258-1993
Director: Dr. Robert Jahn.
Laboratory Manager: Brenda J. Dunne.
Operations Coordinator: Roger D. Nelson.
Laboratory, sporadic technical publications.

Rhine Research Center (RRC)

http://www.rhine.org
2741 Campus Walk Ave., Bldg. 500,
Durham, NC 27705 USA
Phone: 1-919-688-8241; Fax: 1-919-683-4338
Research and education programs are conducted by
the Institute for Parapsychology.
Executive Director: Dr. Sally Feather.
Director of Research: Dr. John Palmer.
Library, introductory material, summer study program. Publications: *Journal of Parapsychology.*

Society for Psychical Research (SPR)

http://www.spr.ac.uk
49 Marloes Road, Kensington,
London W8 6LA, England
Phone & Fax: 44-20-7937-8984
President: Professor Bernard Carr.
Membership organization. Lectures, library,
research grants.
Publications: *Journal of the Society for Psychical
Research, Proceedings of the Society for Psychical
Research, Paranormal Review.*

Society for Scientific Exploration (SSE)
http://www.scientificexploration.org
University of Virginia, PO Box 3818,
Charlottesville, VA 22903-0818 USA
President: Prof. Charles Tolbert.
Secretary: Prof. Laurence W. Fredrick.
Membership organization. Annual meeting.
Publications: *Journal of Scientific Exploration, The Explorer.*

Spiritual Emergence Network (SEN)
http://www.senatciis.org
California Institute of Integral Studies
1453 Mission Street, San Francisco, CA 94103 USA
Phone: 1-408-462-0902
Founders: Dr. Stanislav Grof & Christina Grof.
Director: Karen Trueheart.
Provides information, counseling, and referral services to people experiencing psychospiritual crisis, workshops, conferences.

Spiritual Frontiers Fellowship International (SFFI)
http://www.spiritualfrontiers.org
PO Box 7868, Philadelphia, PA 19101 USA
Phone: 1-215-222-1991
Executive director: Dr. Elizabeth W. Fenske.
Membership organization with local chapters throughout USA. Conferences, lectures, workshops.
Publications: *Spiritual Frontiers, SFFI Newsletter.*

Anthropology of Consciousness
http://aaanet.org
Pub.: Society for the Anthropology of Conscious-
ness (a unit of the American Anthropological
Association), 4350 North Fairfax Drive,
Suite 640, Arlington, VA 22203 USA. Quarterly.
Articles, book reviews, conference reports, and soci-
ety news.

Australian Journal of Parapsychology
http://www.aiprinc.org/journal.htmlpub
Pub.: Australian Institute of Parapsychological
Research (AIPR). PO Box 176, Annandale
NSW 2038, Australia. Annual.
Research and general articles on various areas of
parapsychology.

Christian Parapsychologist
Pub.: Churches' Fellowship for Psychical and Spiritual Studies, South Road, North Somercotes, Nr.
Louth, Lincolnshire LN11 7PT England. Quarterly.
Articles, notes and book reviews with emphasis on
the relationship of religion and spirituality to psychic phenomena.

European Journal of Parapsychology
http://www.psy.gu.se/ejp.htm
Pub.: c/o Department of Psychology, University of
Göteborg, Box 500, SE 405 30 Göteborg, Sweden.
Annual.
Research reports, theoretical presentations, and his-
torical articles. In English.

Exceptional Human Experience
http://www.ehe.org/display/ehe-page.cfm?D=74
(formerly *Parapsychology Abstracts International*).
Pub.: Exceptional Human Experience Network, 414
Rockledge Road, New Bern, NC 28562 USA.
Semi-annual.
Abstracts of recent articles found in both periodicals
and books, original articles, experiences and com-
mentaries.

Fate
http://www.fatemag.com
Pub.: Fate Magazine, Inc., PO Box 460, Lakeville,
MN 55044-0460 USA. Bimonthly
Popular articles about different aspects of the para-
normal. Accounts of psychic experiences.

International Journal of Parapsychology
http://www.parapsychology.org/dynamic/
pubs.ijp
Pub.: Parapsychology Foundation, P. O . Box 1562,
New York, NY 10021-0043 USA. Biannual.
Research and general articles, film reviews and
excerpts of classics of psychical research literature.

IONS Review
http://www.noetic.org/ions/publications/
review.asp
Pub.: Institute of Noetic Sciences, 475 Gate Five
Road, Suite 300, PO Box 909, Sausalito,
CA 94966-0909 USA. Quarterly.
Articles focusing on interdisciplinary approaches to
the study of mind, book reviews, and Institute
news.

Journal of International Society of Life Information Science
http://www.ai-gakkai.or.jp/islis/en/
islis.htm#journal
Pub.: International Society of Life Information
Science, c/o Yamamoto Bio-Emission Laboratory,
National Institute of Radiological Sciences (NIRS),
9-1, Anagawa-4, Inage-ku, Chiba-shi 263-8555
Japan. Biannual.
Research papers on the detection of chi energy and
healing.

Journal of Near-Death Studies
http://www.kluweronline.com/issn/0891-4494
Pub.: Kluwer Academic, for the International
Association of Near-Death Studies,
PO Box 502, East Windsor Hill,
CT 06028-0502 USA. Quarterly.
Research reports, conceptual and theoretical discussion of the near-death experience.

Journal of Parapsychology
http://www.rhine.org/journal.shtml
Pub.: Parapsychology Press, 2741 Campus Walk
Avenue, Bldg. 500, Durham, NC 27705 USA. (Subsidiary of the Rhine Research Center) Quarterly.
Research reports, mainly experimental, theoretical
articles, abstracts, book reviews, and
correspondence.

Journal of Religion and Psychical Research
Pub.: Academy of Religion and Psychical Research,
Box 614, Bloomfield, CT 06002-0614 USA. Quarterly.
Articles discussing religion and its relationship to
psi, book reviews, and announcements.

Journal of Scientific Exploration
http://www.scientificexploration.org/jse.html
Pub.: Society for Scientific Exploration, by Allen
Marketing & Management, 810 E. Tenth St.,
P. O. Box 1897, Lawrence, KS 66044-8897 USA.
Quarterly.
Articles, research reports, book reviews, correspondence, and news items focusing on the areas of science considered anomalous.

Journal of the American Society for Psychical Research
http://www.aspr.com/jaspr.htm
Pub.: ASPR, 5 W. 73rd St., New York, NY
10023 USA. Quarterly.
Experimental reports, survey articles, case studies, book reviews, and correspondence.

Journal of the Society for Psychical Research
http://www.spr.ac.uk/journal.html
Pub.: SPR, 49 Marloes Road, Kensington, London
W8 6LA, England. Quarterly.
Articles, research reports, book reviews, correspondence, and news notes.

Luce e Ombra
http://www2.comune.bologna.it/bologna/
fbibbdb/evleo.htm
Pub.: Fondazione Biblioteca Bozzano-De Boni,
Via Guglielmo Marconi 8, 40122 Bologna, Italy.
Articles on mediumship, spontaneous phenomena
and survival of bodily death.

Metapsichica
http://www.elemaya.com/Aism/default.htm
Pub.: Associazione Italiana Scientifica di Metapsichica, Via Pestalozzi 4, 20143 Milan, Italy. Annual.
Research reports and articles about all aspects of
parapsychology.

Paranormal Review
http://www.spr.ac.uk/review.html
Pub.: SPR, 49 Marloes Road, Kensington, London
W8 6LA, England. Quarterly.
Magazine featuring articles, experiences, abstracts,
and notices of the Society's activities.

Parapsychology Review
http://www.parapsychology.org
Pub.: Parapsychology Foundation, Inc., 228 East 71st
Street, New York, NY 10021 USA.
Bimonthly. Ceased publication March 1990 but back
issues are still available. General articles, including
discussions of education and the state of
parapsychology.
Articles, research and conference reports, book
reviews, and news notes.

Proceedings of the Society for Psychical Research
http://www.spr.ac.uk
Pub.: SPR, 49 Marloes Road, Kensington, London
W8 6LA, England. Irregularly published.
Comprehensive essays and research reports.

Quaderni di Parapsicologia
http://digilander.iol.it/cspbologna/csp-new1/
QP/QP.htm
Pub.: Centro Studi Parapsicologici,
Via Valeriani 39, 40134 Bologna, Italy. Annual.
Research reports and review articles covering all
aspects of parapsychology.

Research in Parapsychology
http://www.scarecrowpress.com [Proceedings of
the annual convention of the Parapsychological
Association Inc.]
Pub.: Scarecrow Press, Lanham, MD 20706 USA.
Published from 1972 to 1993. Back numbers
available.
Reports of current research presented at the annual
conventions of the Parapsychological Association in
longer abstract form, with Presidential and Invited
addresses in full.

Revista Argentina de Psicología Paranormal
http://www.alipsi.com.ar/rapp.htm
Pub.: Instituto de Psicología Paranormal, Salta 2015
(1137), Capital Federal, Buenos Aires, Argentina.
Biannual.
Research reports and review articles of practically
all areas of parapsychology.

Revista Virtual de Pesquisa Psi
http://www.pucsp.br/~cos-puc/cepe/intercon/
revista/revista.htm
Pub.: Inter Psi: Grupo de Estudo de Semiótica,
Interconectividade e Consciência, Centro de
Estudos Peirceanos, Programa de Pós Graduação
em Comunicação e Semiótica, PUC-SP,
São Paulo, Brasil.
Occasional new articles. Articles on general aspects
of parapsychology.

Skeptic
http://www.skeptic.com
Pub.: Millennium Press, PO Box 338, Altadena, CA
91001 USA. Quarterly.
Articles, review essays, and abstracts on controversial claims in the physical, biological, and social sciences.

The Skeptic
http://www.skeptic.org.uk
Pub.: Anomalistic Psychology Research Unit,
Department of Psychology, Goldsmith College,
University of London, New Cross, London
SE14 6NW England. Quarterly.
Articles about skeptical perspective of different
areas of the paranormal.

Skeptical Inquirer
http://www.csicop.org/si
Pub.: Committee for the Scientific Investigation of
Claims of the Paranormal, PO Box 703, Amherst,
NY 14226-0703 USA. Bimonthly.
Articles, news items, book reviews, and bibliogra-
phies generally critical of the paranormal.

Subtle Energies and Energy Medicine
http://www.issseem.org/journal.html
Pub.: International Society for the Study of Subtle
Energies and Energy Medicine,
11005 Ralston Rd., #100D, Arvada, CO 80004 USA.
Research and conceptual papers on the concept of
subtle energy and its use in healing.

Venture Inward
Pub.: Association for Research and Enlightenment,
215 67th St., Virginia Beach, VA 23451-2061 USA.
Bimonthly.
Magazine with articles on parapsychology and con-
sciousness and news information from the Associa-
tion for Research and Enlightenment, founded by
Edgar Cayce.

Zeitschrift für Parapsychologie und Grenzgebiete der
Psychologie
Pub.: Institut für Grenzgebiete der Psychologie und
Psychohygiene (IGPP), Wilhelmstrasse 3a, D79098
Freiburg im Breisgau, Germany. Annual.
Research reports, historical and philosophical
papers.

❖ Appendix D
A Selection of Terms from Dr. Michael A. Thalbourne's *Glossary of Terms Used in Parapsychology**

Agent

In a test of *general extrasensory perception*, the individual (human or animal) who looks at the information constituting the *target* and who is said to "send" or "transmit" that information to a *percipient*; in a test of *telepathy*, and in cases of *spontaneous extrasensory perception*, the individual about whose mental states information is acquired by a percipient; the term is very occasionally used to refer to the *subject* in a test of *psychokinesis* or the *focus* in a *poltergeist* case. [From the Latin *agens (agentis)*, derived from *agere*, "to drive, do"]

Alpha

In the context of brain science: a distinctive brain-rhythm or brain-wave which occurs mainly in the occipital region of the cortex, and which is correlated, on the psychological level, with feelings of drowsiness, relaxation and disengaged attention on the part of the *subject*; it is of relatively high amplitude, and has a frequency range of between 8 and 13 Hz (cycles per second); of *parapsychological* interest as a

* Thalbourne, M. A. (2002). *A Glossary of Terms Used in Parapsychology.* New York: Puente Publications. The italicization of words in the selection that follows indicates that these words are defined as terms either in this section or in Thalbourne's larger glossary.

possible physiological indicator of a *psi-conducive* condition in the subject. [From the Greek *alpha*, first letter of the Greek alphabet, symbolized]

Altered State[s] of Consciousness (ASC)

Expression popularized by Charles T. Tart which can refer to virtually any mental state differing from that of the normal waking condition; of *parapsychological* interest as possibly *psi-conducive* states; they include dreaming, *hypnosis, trance, meditation* of the yoga or Zen tradition, the *hypnagogic*-like state induced by the *ganzfeld*, and drug-induced states.

Anomalistic Psychology

Term first used by Leonard Zusne and Warren Jones (1982) to indicate that part of psychology that investigates "anomalistic" psychological phenomena, that is, phenomena which have tended to be explained in terms of the *paranormal*, the supernatural, magic, or the *occult*; the term is also meant to include belief in UFOs, in astrology, and in such creatures as the Loch Ness Monster.

Anomalous

Having the quality of an *anomaly*.

Anomaly

Neutral term applied to a phenomenon which implies that the phenomenon is unexpected according to conventional scientific knowledge, but which does not commit the user to any particular type of explanation; sometimes preferred to *"paranormal."*

Anpsi
Term coined by J. B. Rhine to refer to *psi* ability in non-human animals. [Contraction of "animal psi"]

Apparition
An experience usually visual but sometimes in other sense-modalities in which there appears to be present a person or animal (deceased or living) and even inanimate objects such as carriages and other things, who/which is in fact out of the sensory range of the experient; often associated with *spontaneous extrasensory perception*, for example, in connection with an agent who is dying or undergoing some other crisis (in which case, it is likely to be termed a "crisis apparition," or in connection with haunting (in which case, it is likely to be referred to in non-technical contexts as a "ghost")

Take-Away Apparition
An apparition seen by a dying person, which "calls them away" by word, look or gesture.

Apport
A physical object which has been *paranormally* transported into a closed space or container, suggesting the passage of "matter through matter," that is, through intervening solid material objects. Compare *Asport* [From the Latin *apportare*, "to carry to (a place)"]

Archeology, Intuitive
See *Psychic Archeology.*

ASC

See *Altered States of Consciousness.*

Astral Body

An entity said to be an exact, quasi-physical replica or "double" of the individual physical body, which can separate itself from the physical body, either temporarily, as in dreaming or in the *out-of-the-body experience,* or permanently, at the moment of death. Also known as the "etheric" body. [From the Latin *astralis,* derived from *astrum,* "star," derived from the Greek *astron*]

Astral Travel

See *Astral Projection* under *Out-of-[the]-Body Experience.*

Aura

A field of subtle, multicolored, luminous radiations said to surround living bodies as a halo or cocoon; the term is occasionally used to refer to the normal electromagnetic field-forces surrounding the body. [Latin, from the Greek, "breath of air"]

Automatic Writing

A motor *automatism* in which a person's hand writes meaningful statements, but without the writer consciously premeditating the content of what is produced.

Automatism

Any complex sensory or motor activity the details of which are carried out by a person without their conscious awareness or volition, thus constituting instances of dissociation; examples of sensory automatisms are certain visual and auditory hallucinations; examples of motor automatisms are sleep-walking, trance-utterances and automatic writing.

Billet Reading

A test in which the *sitter* writes a question on a piece of paper and seals it in an envelope; the *medium* then attempts to answer the question, and sometimes gives additional information relevant to the sitter, purportedly by *paranormal* means. Compare Token-Object Reading [From the French, blend of *bille*, a "writing," and *bullette*, "certificate" (Dale & White, 1977)]

Bilocation

The phenomenon in which a person's body is seen in two different geographical locations at the same time; also, according to Myers (1903), the *sensation* of being in two different places at once, namely, where one's organism is, and a place distant from it, involving some degree of perception (whether *veridical* or *falsidical*) of the distant scene.

Biofeedback

A technique which enables a person to monitor on-going changes in one of their own physiological processes; as a result of such information, the individual may be able to acquire some degree of control in regulating internal processes normally outside the range of voluntary influence; of *parapsychological* interest mainly in connection with *altered states of con-*

sciousness and with the possibility of controlling the incidence of the *alpha* brain-rhythm.

Allobiofeeback

Term used by William G. Braud (1978) to denote the situation in which one *subject*, A, is attempting to influence, *psychokinetically*, the physiological processes of another person, B, aided by biofeedback to A concerning those processes in B. [From the Greek *allos*, "other," + *bios*, "life," + feedback]

Bio-PK

Term used to refer to *psychokinetic* effects brought about on living systems; examples of such effects would be the *paranormal* speeding up or slowing down of the sprouting of seeds or of the growth of bacteria, the resuscitation of anæsthetized mice, and so on; may also include psychosomatic effects; symbolized "PK-LT" (*"psychokinesis* on living targets") by J. B. Rhine.

Book Test

A test for *survival* sometimes conducted during a *sitting* in an attempt to exclude *telepathy* between *medium* and *sitter* as an explanation for the information *paranormally* acquired by the medium: the *communicator* is requested to transmit a message referring to topics on specified pages of a book that the medium could not have normally seen. (As a noun), the overt response made by the *percipient* in guessing the *target*; in a test of *extrasensory perception*; (as a verb), to make a response or call.

Card-Guessing Experiment

Any test of *extrasensory perception* in which cards are used as *targets*.

Chair Test

A test for *precognition*, associated especially with the Dutch *sensitive* Gerard Croiset but first demonstrated by Pascal Forthuny, a French *psychic*, in which a chair is randomly selected from all those set up for a later public meeting, and the *percipient* describes the appearance, characteristics and events in the life of a person, unknown to them, who will later attend that meeting and occupy that chair.

Chance

The constellation of undefined causal factors which are considered to be irrelevant to the causal relationship under investigation; often spoken of as if it were a single, independent agency; the expression "pure chance" is sometimes used to describe a state characterized by complete unpredictability, that is, an absence of *any* cause-effect relationships. The term "chance" is frequently a short-hand expression for *"mean chance expectation,"* as in *"deviation* from chance."

Channel

A term which became popular in the 1970s. As a noun it refers to a *medium;* as a verb it means to engage in the process of *channeling*.

Channeling

A phenomenon in which, according to Arthur Hastings (1990, p. 99), "a person purports to transmit information or messages directly from a personality or consciousness other than his or her own, usually through *automatic writing* or *trance* speaking; this other personality usually claims to be a nonphysical *spirit* or being."

Clairaudience

Paranormal information expressed as an auditory experience; it is generally considered to be a form or mode of *clairvoyance*. [From the French *clair*, "clear," + *audience*, "hearing," ultimately derived from the Latin *clarus*, "clear," + *audientia*, derived from *audire*, "to hear"]

Clairaudient

Pertaining to, or involving, *clairaudience*.

Clairsentience

Paranormal information expressed as a sensation or feeling; generally considered to be a form of *clairvoyance*. [From the French *clair*, "clear," + *sentience*, "feeling," ultimately derived from the Latin *clarus*, "clear," + *sentiens*, derived from *sentire*, "to feel"]

Clairsentient

As a noun, a person gifted with *clairsentience*; As an adjective, pertaining to or involving clairsentience.

Clairvoyance

Paranormal acquisition of information concerning an object or contempory physical event; in contrast to *telepathy*, the information is assumed to derive directly from an external physical source (such as a concealed photograph), and not from the mind of another person; one particular form of *extrasensory perception,* it is not to be confused with the vulgar interpretation of "clairvoyance" as meaning "knowledge of the future" (for which see *Precognition*).

Clairvoyant

As a noun, a person endowed with a special talent for *clairvoyance*; not to be confused with its colloquial usage meaning "a fortune-teller"; As an adjective, involving or pertaining to clairvoyance.

Cognition

A psychological term covering all the various modes of human information-processing, such as perception, memory, imagination and problem-solving; generally used to denote the process, but occasionally the product. [From the Latin *cognito,* "acquiring of knowledge," derived from *cognoscere,* "to get to know"]

Coincidence; in the paranormal

Two events are said to constitute a coincidence if they occur in such a way as to strike an observer as being highly related as regards their structure or their "meaning"; to dismiss such an occurrence as a "mere coincidence" is to imply the belief that each event arose as a result of quite independent causal chains (that is, they are "acausal") and that no further "meaning" or significance is to be found in this fortuitous concurrence; sometimes, however, a sense of impressiveness is engendered by the belief that the concurrence is so very unlikely as to have been the result of "pure chance" that there must be some cause or reason for the concurrence, thus investing the coincidence with a sense of meaningfulness. See also *Synchronicity.*

Cold Reading

A set of statements purportedly gained by *paranormal* means but which in fact is wholly based on broadly accurate generalizations and/or on information obtained directly from the person seeking the reading, such as can be gleaned from facial gestures, clues in conversation, and so on.

Communicator

A personality, usually manifesting through a *medium*, and claiming to be that of a deceased individual trying to communicate with the living. See also *Drop-in Communicator.*

Control

(i) A personality purporting to be that of some deceased individual, believed to take control of the *medium's* actions and speech during *trance*, and/or who habitually relays messages from the *communicator* to the *sitter.* (ii) In the context of scientific investigation, a control is something (a procedure, condition, object, set of *subjects*, and so on) which is introduced with the purpose of providing a check on (that is, of "controlling for") the influence of unwanted factors.

Crisis Aparition

See under *Apparition.*

Cross-Correspondence

A highly complex series of independent communications delivered *paranormally* (and ostensibly from one or more *discarnate entities*) to two or more geographically separate *mediums* such that the complete message is not clear until the separate fragments are pieced together into a meaningful whole.

Cryptomnesia

Term coined by Theodore Flournoy to refer to a memory of some event or experience which has been forgotten by the conscious mind, and which may appear in awareness without the person recognizing it as a memory; sometimes invoked as a counterhypothesis to apparent *paranormal* awareness. [From the Greek *kryptos*, "hidden," + *mnesis*, "memory"]

Crystal-Gazing

See *Scrying*.

Déjà Vu

French for "already seen," the feeling or illusion of having previously experienced an event or place actually being encountered for the first time; also called "false memory," or "memory without recognition," although the phenomenon could conceivably involve *precognitive* or *clairvoyant* information, in which case Frederic Myers gave it the name *promnesia* [From the Greek *pro*, "prior to," + *mnesis*, "memory"].

Dematerialization

A phenomenon of *physical mediumship* in which living entities (sometimes the *medium's* own body) or inanimate objects — sometimes previously *materialized* — are caused to disappear. Compare *Materialization*.

Dermo-Optical Perception (DOP)

Term used by G. Razran to refer to the ability to discriminate color and brightness by means of touch. Also known as "skin vision," "finger vision," "dermal vision," "digital sight" [From the Latin *digitus*, "finger, toe"], or "cutaneous perception" [From the Latin *cutis*, "skin"]. [From the Greek *derma*, "skin," + *optikos*, "of sight," derived from *opsomai*, "I shall see"]

Diagnosis, Paranormal

The determination of the nature and circumstances of a diseased condition by means of *extrasensory perception*. See also *Healing, Psychic*.

Discarnate Entity

A disembodied being, as opposed to an incarnate one; the surviving personality of a deceased individual or non-human entity; a *spirit*. [From the Latin *dis-*, "away, apart," + *caro (carnis)*, "flesh"]

Dissociation

A process in which a body of awareness (perceptual, memory, physical) becomes separated or blocked from the main center of consciousness; examples are *trance-speaking, automatic writing,* amnesia, *multiple personality,* and so on; thought by some to be a *psi-conducive* state.

Divination

Word sometimes used to refer to the acquiring of *paranormal* information, frequently (but not invariably) by the use of such various practices as tea-leaf reading, palmistry, *scrying*, the *I Ching*, *Tarot* cards and so on.

Divining Rod

See under *Dowsing*.

Doppelgänger

An *apparitional* double or counterpart of a living person. See also *Astral Body; Bilocation* [German for "doublewalker"]

Dowsing

A behavioral *automatism* in which, generally, a "dowsing rod" (also called a divining rod: often a forked twig but sometimes a *pendulum*) is employed to locate subterranean water, oil, and so on, or other concealed items by following the direction in which the rod turns in the user's hands. Some practitioners use their bare hands with no gadget.

Dream, Veridical

An apparently *paranormal* dream, inasmuch as some of the dream details give information about events normally unknowable to the experient.

Drop-in Communicator

Term coined by Ian Stevenson for a *communicator* who appears unbidden at a *sitting*, and who is entirely unknown to the *medium*, *sitters*, or anyone else present.

Ectoplasm

Term introduced into *parapsychology* by Charles Richet to describe the "exteriorized substance" produced out of the bodies of some *physical mediums* and from which *materializations* are sometimes formed. [From the Greek *ektos*, "outside," + *plasma*, "something formed or molded"]

EEG

See *Electroencephalograph*.

Electroencephalograph (EEG)

The mechanical device employed in the technique known as *electroencephalography*.

Electronic Voice Phenomena (EVP)

Phenomena first reported by Raymond Bayless and popularized by Konstantin Raudive, consisting of sounds said to be the faint voices of deceased individuals, recorded on previously unused magnetic tapes.

ESP

See *Extrasensory Perception*.

ESP Cards

A special deck of cards, developed by perceptual psychologist Karl Zener for use by J. B. Rhine in tests of *extrasensory perception*: a standard pack contains 25 cards, each portraying one of five symbols — circle, cross, square, star or wavy lines. Also called *Zener cards*.

Exceptional Human Experience

Expression coined by Rhea White (see, for example, 1994, p. 5) as "an umbrella term for many types of experience generally considered to be *psychic, mystical,* encounter-type experiences, death-related experiences, and experiences at the upper end of the normal range, such as creative inspiration, exceptional human performance, as in sports, literary and aesthetic experiences, and the experience of falling in love."

Experimenter Effect

An experimental outcome which results not from manipulation of the *variable* of interest *per se,* but rather from some aspect of the particular experimenter's behavior, such as unconscious communication to the *subjects,* or possibly even a *psi-mediated* effect working in accord with the experimenter's desire to confirm some hypothesis.

Extrasensory Perception (ESP)

The acquisition of information about, or response to, an external event, object or influence (mental or physical; past, present or future) otherwise than through any of the known sensory channels; used by J. B. Rhine to embrace such phenomena as *telepathy, clairvoyance* and *precognition*; there is some difference of opinion as whether the term ought to be attributed to Rhine, or to Gustav Pagenstecher or Rudolph Tischner, who were using the German equivalent *aussersinnliche Wahrehmung* as early as the 1920s. [From the Latin *extra, "outside of,"* + *sensory*]

Faith Healing

See *Healing, Psychic.*

Fantasy-Proneness

A personality construct first described by Sheryl Wilson and Theodore Barber (1983, p. 340) to refer to a small percentage of the population "who fantasize a large part of the time, [and] who typically 'see,' 'hear,' 'smell,' 'touch' and fully experience what they fantasize"; such persons tend to be able to hallucinate voluntarily, to be excellent hypnotic subjects, to have vivid memories of their life experiences, and to report experiencing *parapsychological* phenomena.

Ganzfeld

Term referring to a special type of environment (or the technique for producing it) consisting of homogenous, unpatterned sensory stimulation: audiovisual ganzfeld may be accomplished by placing translucent hemispheres (for example, halved ping-pong balls) over each eye of the *subject*, with diffused light (frequently red in hue) projected onto them from an external source, together with the playing of unstructured sounds (such as "white" or "pink" noise) into the ears, and generally with the person in a state of bodily comfort; the consequent deprivation of patterned sensory input is said to be conducive to introspection of inwardly-generated impressions, some of which may be *extrasensory* in origin. [From the German for "entire field"]

Manual Ganzfeld

The use of the word "manual" refers to the fact that the *target* selection is carried out by manual access to computer or random number tables as well as the fact that all the important events in the experiment are recorded by hand. Consequently, the technique has limited safeguards against fraud or data selection compared with the *autoganzfeld*.

Autoganzfeld

An implementation of the ganzfeld technique in which many of the key procedural details, such as selection and presentation of the *target* and the recording of the evaluation of the target-response similarity given by the *percipient* are fully automated and computerized, the goal being to reduce as far as possible errors and sensory communication on the part of the human participants.

Geller Effect

The ability to bend metal by *paranormal* means; named after the Israeli stage performer Uri Geller, who was the first person to claim publicly the *metal-bending* ability; the term has been largely superseded by "PK-MB," or, more simply, "metal-bending." See also *Mini-Geller; Psychokinesis.*

General Extrasensory Perception (GESP)

A non-committal technical term used to refer to instances of *extrasensory perception* in which the information *paranormally* acquired may have been derived either from another person's mind (that is, as *telepathy*), or from a physical event or state of affairs (that is, as *clairvoyance*), or even from both sources; experimental *parapsychologists* rarely use the term "telepathy" because of the difficulty, in tests of so-called telepathy, of excluding the possible operation of clairvoyance.

Ghost

As popularly used, this term denotes only the *apparition* of a deceased person, and is not sufficiently precise for use in *psychical research*. [Ashby, 1972]

Glossolalia

Speaking in "tongues," that is, in a language which is either unknown to linguistic science, or completely fabricated; it usually occurs in a religious context or is attributed to religious inspiration, as from the Holy Spirit; not to be confused with *xenoglossy*. [From the Greek *glossa*, "tongue, language," + *lalia*, "chat, gossip, talking," derived from *lalein*, "to make an inarticulate sound"]

Goat

Term originally used by Gertrude Schmeidler (1943) to describe a subject who rejects the possibility that *extrasensory perception* could occur under the conditions of the given experimental situation; this somewhat narrow meaning has been extended to refer also, or alternatively, to persons who do not believe in the existence of *ESP* in general (that is, under *any* conditions!), or even to persons who obtain low scores on various so-called "projective," "scalar" or "checklist" measures of belief in (and/or experience of, different sorts of putative *psi* phenomena. Compare *Sheep*. See *Sheep-Goat Effect*. [Taken from a *New Testament* simile, Matthew 25: 31-33: "But when the Son of Man shall come in his majesty, and all the angels with him, then he will sit on the throne of his glory; and before him will be gathered all the nations, and he will separate them one from another, as the shepherd separates the sheep from the goats; and he will set the sheep on his right hand, but the goats on the left."]

Hallucination

An experience having the same phenomenological characteristics as a sense-perception, and which may lead the experient to suppose the presence of an external physical object as the cause of that experience, but in which, in fact, there is no such object present.

Haunting

The more or less regular occurrence of paranormal phenomena associated with a particular locality (especially a building) and usually attributed to the activities of a *discarnate entity*; the phenomena may include *apparitions, poltergeist* disturbances, cold drafts, sounds of steps and voices, and various odors.

Healing, Psychic

Healing apparently brought about by such non-medical means as prayer, the "laying on of hands," Psychic healing; immersion at a religious shrine, and so on, and inexplicable according to contemporary medical science; not to be confused with merely unconventional medicine.

Hypnagogic State

Term referring to the transitional state of consciousness experienced while falling asleep, sometimes characterized by vivid hallucinations or imagery of varying degrees of bizarreness; sometimes used to refer also to the similar state of awareness experienced during the process of waking up. Compare *Hypnopompic State* [From the Greek *hypnos,* "sleep," + *agogos,* "leading"]

Hypnopompic State

Term coined by Frederic Myers to refer to the transitional state of consciousness experienced while waking from sleep; the term *"hypnagogic"* is sometimes used to refer to this state also. [From the Greek *hypnos,* "sleep," + *pompos,* "escort, guide"]

Hypnosis

A condition or state, commonly resembling sleep, which is accompanied by narrowing of the range of attention, is characterized by marked susceptibility to suggestion, and can be artificially induced.

I Ching

Also known as the *Book of Change[s],* a book of great antiquity originating in China and used principally as a tool for *divination.* It consists of 64 unique "hexagrams," or six-line structures, each line carrying a piece of binary information and known as a yin line or a yang line. Each hexagram has attached to it a distinctly different *reading* describing an outcome or human situation. The user asks a question, and employs either yarrow stalks (the traditional method) or three coins (the more usual method in modern times) to generate in a "random" way a particular hexagram, the reading for which, it is claimed, is the answer to the user's question [pronounced "Yee Jing"].

Intuition

Somewhat ill-defined term referring to the faculty of coming to an idea *directly,* by means other than those of reasoning and intellect, and indeed often outside of all conscious processes; the source of these messages is often said to be in the normal, mundane, unconscious, but it is often also said to be the result of *mystical* or *paranormal* processes. The word sometimes refers to the *process*, sometimes to the *product* of intuition. [From the Latin *intueri*, "to look at, contemplate"]

Intuitive Archeology

See *Psychic Archeology.*

Judging

The process whereby a rating or a rank-score (that is, "1st," "2nd," "3rd," and so on) is awarded to one or more *responses* produced (or *targets* used) in a *free-response test* of *extrasensory perception,* in accordance with the degree of correspondence obtaining between them or one or more targets (or responses); also, the attempt to match, under *blind* conditions, a set of targets with a set of responses.

Kirlian Photography

A type of high-voltage, high-frequency photography, developed in the Soviet Union by Semyon Davidovich Kirlian, which records on photographic film the so-called "corona discharge" of an object caused by ionization of the field surrounding that object; it is claimed by some that this process indicates the existence of hitherto unknown radiations or energy fields such as "bioplasma" or the "psychic aura."

Laying-on-of-Hands

See under *Healing, Psychic.*

Levitation

The raising or suspension of persons or objects into the air without any apparent agency as required by known physical laws of motion and gravity.

Lucid Dream

A dream in which the dreamer is conscious of the fact that they are dreaming.

Luminous Phenomena

The *paranormal* production of light phenomena, generally in the presence of certain *physical mediums.*

Macro-PK

See under *Psychokinesis.*

Meditation

A broad term embracing a number of techniques for achieving various altered states of awareness, with some of these altered states resulting in the ecstatic qualities of so-called "peak experience;" most meditative techniques are ways of learning to still the agitation of the mind so that more subtle and valuable aspects of self and reality may be perceived; some techniques involve concentration, in which attention is focused on a particular object and restrained from wandering, while others involve giving one's total attention to whatever spontaneously happens, with no attempt to control or focus attention.

Medium

A predominantly *Spiritualistic* term applied to a person who regularly, and to a greater or lesser extent at will, is involved in the production of *psi* in the form *mental* and/or *physical phenomena*. See also *Communicator; Control; Sensitive; Trance; Apport; Ectoplasm; Levitation.*

Mentalism

The practice of simulating *telepathy*, performed for the purpose of entertainment.

Mesmerism

The original term for what has since become known as "hypnotism," named after the Austrian physician Franz Anton Mesmer (1733-1815), who believed that it involved the transfer from operator to patient of a subtle fluid, force or energy known as "animal magnetism."

Metal-Bender

A person capable of performing *psychokinetic metal-bending.*

Metal-Bending

See *Psychokinetic Metal-bending.*

Metapsychics

Anglicization of a French term coined by Charles Richet as an alternative designation for the subject matter of *parapsychology.* [From the Greek *meta*, indicating change of condition, + *psychikos*, "of the soul, mental"]

Micro-PK

See under *Psychokinesis.*

Mini-Geller

A child or young person who can to some extent duplicate by *paranormal* means the *metal-bending* feats of Uri Geller. See also *Geller Effect.*

Muscle-Reading

A phenomena which mimics *telepathy,* in which a person is able, for example, to find a hidden object by means of physical contact with the person who knows its whereabouts, probably due to subtle muscular cues that the latter provides unconsciously; also known as "Cumberlandism," after Stuart Cumberland, a nineteenth century practitioner of this art.

Mystical Experience

An experience which, according to Michael A. Thalbourne (1991a, 1991b), consists of a majority of the following features: it tends to be sudden in onset, joyful, and difficult to verbalize; it involves a sense of perceiving the purpose of existence; an insight into "the harmony of things;" a perception of an ultimate unity — of oneness; transcendence of the ego; an utter conviction of immortality; and it tends to be temporary, authoritative and to be attributed supreme value. Some people interpret the mystical experience as an experience of unity with God.

NDE

See *Near-Death Experience.*

NDEr

A person who has undergone a *near-death experience.*

Near-Death Experience (NDE)

Term applied to experiences undergone by persons who either seem to be at the point of death (or who are even formally declared dead) but then recover, or who narrowly escape death (as in a motor car accident) without being seriously injured; it has been suggested that there is, upon coming close to death, a "core" NDE made up of certain common elements, such as a feeling of indescribable peace, a sense of being out of one's body, a movement into a dark void or down a tunnel, seeing a brilliant light, and entering that light; there may also be reported the experience of so-called "panoramic memory" (the "life review"), the encountering of an "unseen presence," or being greeted by deceased relatives or religious figures. See also *Deathbed Experience.*

OBE

See *Out-of-[the]-Body Experience.*

OBEr

A person who undergoes an out-of-[the]-body experience.

Occult

Term referring to certain reputed sciences and practices such as magic, astrology, witchcraft, sorcery, and so on, involving esoteric knowledge or the employment of mysterious agencies; not to be confused with scientific *parapsychology.* [From the Latin *occultus*, "covered over, concealed"]

Ouija Board

A device consisting of a board marked with words, alphabetical letters and numerals, together with a smaller board on three legs, one of which serves as a pointer; the device is employed to spell out messages, answers, and so on, by having the fingers of one or more persons rest lightly upon the pointer, which moves over the larger board and stops at the various markings; some of these messages may be *extrasensory* in origin. Nowadays an upturned glass is frequently used to spell out messages. See also *Planchette* [From the French *oui* + German *ja*, both meaning "yes"]

Out-of-[the]-Body Experience (OBE, or OOBE)

An experience, either spontaneous or induced, in which one's center of consciousness seems to be in a spatial location outside of one's physical body; Celia Green distinguishes two types of such "ecsomatic" [From the Greek *ek*, "out of," + *soma*, "body"] experiences: the "parasomatic" [From the Greek *para*, "along side of"] in which the person appears to themselves to possess a duplicate body, sometimes connected to the physical body by a "silver cord;" and the "asomatic" [From the Greek *a-*, "without"] in which they feel thernselves to be entirely bodiless; in either case, many experients claim to perceive their physical bodies lying inert, to see and hear people while remaining unperceived themselves, and to perceive objects and events normally beyond the range of their physical senses; of special interest to parapsychologists on account of its alleged connection with *clairvoyance*, and to students of *survival* as providing an example of what disembodied existence could be like. The term "OBE" is preferred by parapsychologists for the phenomena also known as *"astral projection," "traveling clairvoyance."* See also *Astral Body.* [Dale & White, 1977]

ESP Projection

Term coined by Hornell Hart to refer to a type of OBE in which the person "projecting" their consciousness out of their body actually feels that they are out of their body, may be seen by other people at a distant point, and afterwards reports a *veridical* description of what he or she observed at that point.

Paranormal

Term applied to any phenomenon which in one or more respects exceeds the limits of what is deemed physically possible on current scientific assumptions; often used as a synonym for *"psychic," "parapsychological," "attibutable to psi,"* or even "miraculous" (although shorn of religious overtones). See also *Basic Limiting Principles.* [From the Greek *para,* "beside, beyond," + *normal*]

Paraphysics

Pertaining to *paraphysics;* synonym for "psychokinetic."

Parapsychological

Involving or pertaining to *parapsychology* or *paranormal* processes.

Parapsychology

Term coined in German by Max Dessoir (1889) and adopted by J. B. Rhine in English to refer to the scientific study of *paranormal* or *ostensibly* paranormal phenomena, that is, *psi;* except in Britain, the term has largely superseded the older expression *"psychical research;"* used by some to refer to the experimental approach to the field. [From the Greek *para,* "beside, beyond," + *psychology,* derived from the Greek *psyche,* "soul, mind," + *logos* "rational discussion"]

Past-Life Regression

A process in which a hypnotized person is mentally "taken back" (or "regressed") by the *hypnotist* to one or more apparent previous lifetimes, thus suggesting *reincarnation.*

Percipient

Broadly speaking, someone who perceives or who has a perception-like experience, in particular, the person who experiences or "receives" an *extrasensory* influence or impression; also one who is tested for ESP ability. Compare *Agent; Subject.* [From the Latin *percipiens (percipientis),* derived from *percipere,* "to receive, understand"]

Phantasm

Any hallucinatory sensory impression, whatever sense may happen to be affected. See also *Apparition; Hallucination.* [From the Greek *phantasma,* "appearance, image, phantom"] [Nash, 1978]

Photography, Paranormal

The *paranormal* production of images on photographic film; also known as "thoughtography," a term used to describe the experiments of Tomokichi Fukurai (1931) but adopted by Jule Eisenbud to describe the phenomena produced by Ted Serios, as if mental images were "projected" onto the film. See also *Thoughtography; Spirit Photography.*

PK

See *Psychokinesis.*

Poltergeist

A disturbance characterized by bizarre physical effects of *paranormal* origin, suggesting mischievous or destructive intent: these phenomena include the unexplained movement or breakage of objects, loud *raps*, the lighting of fires, and occasionally personal injury to people; in contrast to a *haunting*, the phenomena often seem to depend upon the presence of a particular living individual, called the "focus," frequently an adolescent or child; and *apparitions* are rarely seen. [German: literally, "noisy ghost"]

Possession

The complete control, by an *ostensible discarnate entity*, of the body of a living person.

Post-Mortem Communication

A communication or message said to be from a deceased to a living person, usually delivered through a *medium*.

Precognition

A form of *extrasensory perception* in which the *target* is some future event that cannot be deduced from normally known data in the present. Compare *Retrocognition*. [From the Latin *præ-*, "prior to," + *cognitio*, "a getting to know"]

Premonition

A feeling or impression that something is about to happen, especially something ominous or dire, yet about which no normal information is available. See *Precognition*. [From the Latin *præ*, "prior to," + *monitio*, "warning"]

Psi (Ψ)

A general blanket term, proposed by B. P. Wiesner and seconded by R. H. Thouless (1942), and used either as a noun or adjective to identify *paranormal* processes and paranormal causation; the two main categories of *psi* are *psi-gamma* (paranormal cognition; *extrasensory perception*) and *psi-kappa* (paranormal action; *psychokinesis*), although the purpose of the term "psi" is to suggest that they might simply be different aspects of a single process, rather than distinct and essentially different processes. Strictly speaking "psi" also applies to *survival* of death. Some thinkers prefer to use "psi" as a purely descriptive term for *anomalous* outcomes, as suggested by Palmer (1986, p. 139), who defines it as "a correspondence between the cognitive or physiological activity of an organism and events in its external environment that is anomalous with respect to generally accepted *basic limiting principles* of nature such as those articulated by C. D. Broad." [From the Greek, *psi*, twenty-third letter of the Greek alphabet; from the Greek *psyche*, "mind, soul"]

Psi-Conducive

Favorable to, or facilitative of, the occurrence of *psi*, whether it be manifested as *psi-hitting* or *psi-missing*.

Psi-Hitting

The use of *psi* in such a way that the *target* at which the *subject* is aiming is "hit" (that is, correctly responded to, in a test of *extrasensory perception;* or influenced, in a test of *psychokinesis*), more frequently than would be expected if only chance were operating; the term is also sometimes used, misleadingly, to refer merely to *non-significant* positive scoring. Hence, "psi-hitter," a subject who exhibits a tendency to psi-hit. Compare *Psi-Missing*. [Abbreviated to ΨH by James Carpenter]

Psi-Missing

The use of *psi* in such a way that the *target* at which the *subject* is aiming is "missed" (that is, responded to incorrectly, in a test of *extrasensory perception;* or influenced in a direction contrary to aim, in a test of *psychokinesis*) more frequently than would be expected if only *chance* were operating; the term is also sometimes used, misleadingly, to refer simply to *non-significant* negative scoring. Hence, "psi-misser," a subject who displays a tendency to psi-miss. Compare *Psi-Hitting*. [Abbreviated to ΨM by James Carpenter]

Psi Phenomenon

Any event which results from, or is an instance of, the operation of *psi*; examples are the forms of *extrasensory perception* and *psychokinesis*.

Psychic(al)

As a noun, "psychic" refers to an individual who possesses *psi* ability of some kind and to a relatively high degree; as an adjective, it is nowadays applied to *paranormal* events, abilities, research, and so on, and thus means "concerning or involving psi," or "*parapsychological.*" [From the Greek *psychikos*, "of the soul, mental," derived from *psyche*, "soul, mind"]

Psychical Research

The original term for "*parapsychology,*" still widely used, especially in Britain.

Psychic Archeology
Archeological research which is pursued with the assistance of a *sensitive* or other source of *paranormal* information.

Psychic Healing
See *Healing, Psychic.*

Psychic Photography
See *Photography, Paranormal.*

Psychic Surgery
A form of *psychic healing* practiced particularly in the Philippines, in which diseased tissue are said to be removed without the use of surgical instruments, and bleeding, infection, and the like, are inhibited *paranormally.* The term is also used of surgery in which the surgeon operates while in a *trance,* as performed by J. Arigo and other Brasilian exponents of this pratice, usually using unsterilized knives as scalpels.

Psychokinesis
Paranormal action; term coined by Henry Holt and adopted by J. B. Rhine to refer to the direct influence of mind on a physical system that cannot be entirely accounted for by the mediation of any known physical energy. See also *Psi-Kappa* under *Psi; Retroactive PK; Recurrent Spontaneous Psychokinesis.* [From the Greek *psyche,* "mind, soul," + *kinesis,* "a moving, disturbance,"* derived from *kinein,* "to set in motion"

Psychokinetic Metal-Bending (PK-MB)

A *psychokinetic* effect in which metallic objects such as keys, cutlery and so on are subjected to more or less permanent deformation or other structural change.

Psychometry

Term coined by Joseph Rodes Buchanan (1893) to refer to the practice in which *sensitives* hold an object in their hands and obtain *paranormal* information about the object or its owner; owing to the confusion with a psychological term, "psychometry" has in recent years been superseded by "token-object reading." [From the Greek *psyche*, "soul, mind," + *metrein*, "to measure"]

Psychotronics

Czech term for *"parapsychology"* (excluding the study of survival), but embracing certain phenomena that are not now generally accepted as *parapsychological*. According to Larissa Vilenskaya (1983, p. 107), the term was first proposed with the analogy of "bionics" in mind, to refer to " the field dealing with the construction of devices capable of enhancing and/or reproducing certain psi phenomena (such as *psychokinesis* in the case of 'psychotronic generators' developed by Robert Pavlita) and later embraced some other phenomena." [Dale & White, 1977]

Qualitative Experiment

(i) Any test for *extrasensory perception* which uses *target* material and forms of *response* which do not allow a definite *probability-value* to be attached to the response items made; examples are most *free-response tests*, tests of *psychometry*, *mediumistic* utterances, and so on; statistical evaluation of such data must therefore proceed in an indirect fashion, by assigning a probability-value to the matching-performance of a judge; (ii) Any attempt to demonstrate qualitative phenomena. Compare *Quantitative Experiment*. [Ultimately derived from the Latin *qualis*, "what kind of?"]

Quantitative Experiment

Any test for *psi* which uses *targets* each of which has a specific prescribed *value* for the *probability* of its occurrence; such a test therefore allows for direct statistical evaluation of the results obtained. See also *Forced-Choice Test*. Compare *Qualitative Experiment*. [Ultimately derived from the Latin *quantus*, "how great, how much?"]

Radionics

A term which has largely supplanted "radiæsthesia" in English usage.

Random Number Generator (RNG)

An apparatus (typically electronic) incorporating an element (based on such processes as radioactive decay or random "noise") and capable of generating a random sequence of outputs; used in tests of *psi* for generating *target* sequences, and in tests of *psychokinesis* may itself be the target system which the *subject* is required to influence, that is, by "biasing" the particular number or event output; a *binary* RNG has two equally-probable outputs; the term "RNG" is increasingly being used to refer to any system which produces naturally random outputs, such as bouncing dice, radioactive decay, or even, perhaps, the brain.

Raps

Percussive sounds, often tapping out an intelligible message, sometimes said to be produced by *paranormal* means.

Raudive Voice Phenomena

See *Electronic Voice Phenomena.*

Reading

The statements made by a *sensitive* (or as a result of the process of *divination*) in the course of an attempt to obtain paranormal information or "messages."

Receiver

An expression which is less technical than *"percipient,"* used to indicate the subject designated as the "recipient" of telepathic information. Compare *Sender.*

Recurrent Spontaneous Psychokinesis (RSPK)

Expression coined by William G. Roll to refer to *paranormal* physical effects which occur repeatedly over a period of time, especially used as a neutral description of *poltergeist* disturbances. See also *Psychokinesis.*

Reincarnation

A form of survival in which the human soul, or some aspects of self, is, after the death of the body, reborn into a new body, this process being repeated throughout many lives. See also *Rebirth*. [From the Latin *re-*, "again," + *in-*, "into," + *caro (carnis)*, "flesh"]

Remote Viewing

A neutral term for *general extrasensory perception* introduced Russell Targ and Harold Puthoff (1974), especially in the context of an experimental design in which a *percipient* attempts to describe the surroundings of a geographically distant *agent*.

Associational Remote Viewing (ARV)

As described by Targ (1983), a form of remote viewing in which the area where a desired item might be located is divided up into a finite number of discrete locations; each of the possible locations, or addresses, is associated or linked with a laboratory-based *token object* or picture (such as of the Golden Gate Bridge); the viewer is then asked to describe the associated target-object. thereby indirectly choosing a particular target-location or address.

Retroactive PK

Psychokinesis occurring in such a way as to be an instance of *retroactive causation*; to say that event A was caused by retroactive PK is to say that A would not have happened in the way that it did had it not been for a later PK effort exerted so as to influence it. Sometimes abbreviated to "retro-PK;" also referred to as "backward PK" or "time-displaced PK."

Retrocognition

Term coined by Frederic Myers to refer to a form of *extrasensory perception* in which the *target* is some past event which could not have been learned or inferred by normal means. Compare *Precognition* [From the Latin *retro*, "backward, behind," + *cognitio*, "a getting to know"]

Revenant

An apparition of a deceased person. [From the French *revenir*, ultimately derived from the Latin *revenire*, "to come back"]

RSPK

See *Recurrent Spontaneous Psychokinesis*.

Scrying

A technique for obtaining *paranormal* impressions by staring into a crystal ball, pool of water, coffee grounds, tea leaves and so on, which causes the practitioner to experience images or exteriorized *hallucinations*. [Variant of *descry*]

Seance

A meeting of one or more persons, generally, but not always, with a medium, for the purpose of eliciting *physical phenomena* and/or for receiving communications from the deceased; the term has also been used without *Spiritualistic* connotations, that is, to refer to the purpose of getting together to observe phenomena, without the intent to communicate with the dead. Also called a *"sitting"* or *"session."* [From the French, derived from the Old French *seoir*, "to sit," ultimately derived from the Latin *sedere*, "to sit"]

Second Sight
Concept used in the Celtic folklore of the *supernatural*, and encompassing what would today be referred to as "psychic ability." Also sometimes called "deuteroscopy." [From the Greek *deuteros*, "second," + *skopia*, derived from *skopein*, "to look at"]

Sender
Less technical expression than "agent," used to denote the person or *subject* designated as the "transmitter" of *telepathic* information. Compare *Receiver*.

Sensitive
A person who frequently experiences *extrasensory perception* and who can sometimes induce it at will. Compare *Medium*.

Shaman
A tribal *medium*, witch-doctor, or priest accredited with supernatural powers as originally exemplified by Siberian tribes. [From the German *Schamane*, derived from the Russian *shaman*, derived from *Tungusic samân*]

Sheep
Term originally used by Gertrude Schmeidler (1943) to describe a *subject* who does not reject the possibility that *extrasensory perception* could occur under the conditions of the given experimental situation; this somewhat narrow meaning has been extended to refer also, tentatively,

to persons who believe that *ESP* exists as a genuine phenomenon, or even to persons who obtain high scores on various so-called "projective," "scalar," or "checklist" measures of belief in (and/or experience of) different sorts of putative *psi* phenomena. Compare *Goat*. See also *Sheep-Goat Effect*. [Taken from the *New Testament* simile, Matthew 25: 31-33: "But when the Son of Man shall come in his majesty, and all the angels with him, then he will sit on the throne of his glory; and before him will be gathered all the nations, and he will separate them one from another, as the shepherd separates the sheep from the goats; and he will set the sheep on his right hand, but the goats on the left."]

Super-Sheep (or White Sheep)

Term introduced by John Beloff and David Bate (1970) to describe a subject who is sure that their score on a test of *extrasensory perception* will be high, by virtue of their own psychic ability.

Sheep-Goat Effect (SGE)

Term first used by Gertrude Schmeidler to describe the relationship between acceptance of the possibility of *extrasensory perception* occurring under the given experimental conditions, and the level of scoring actually achieved on that *ESP* test: subjects who do not reject the possibility ("*sheep*") tend to score above *chance*, those rejecting the possibility ("*goats*") at or below chance; the terms "sheep" and "goat" are nowadays often used in a more extended sense, and "sheep-goat effect" may thus refer to any *significant* scoring difference between these two groups as defined by the experimenter.

Sitter

A person who sits with a *medium* at a *seance* and who receives a communication through the medium.

Sitter Group

As defined by Kenneth Batcheldor (1984, p. 105), "a small, semi-informal group that seeks to develop *paranormal* physical phenomena by meeting repeatedly under conditions that resemble those of a Victorian seance. No spiritistic assumptions are made, however, and the phenomena — such as rapping noises and *levitation* of tables — insofar as they may be paranormal are interpreted in terms of the PK abilities of the sitters."

Sitting

A *session* or interview with a *medium*, generally by an individual or a small number of people, and often for the purpose of obtaining communications from the deceased; also termed a "seance."

Absent (or Proxy) Sitting

A sitting at which the person desiring to receive a communication via a medium absents themselves from the actual sitting and is represented by another person, called a *"proxy sitter."*

Skin Vision

See *Dermo-Optical Perception.*

Speaking in Tongues
See *Glossolalia; Xenoglossy.*

Spirit
A discarnate entity.

Spirit Hypothesis
The theory that individual consciousness survives the death of the body in the form of a *spirit*, and that it may be communicated with by living persons, especially via a *medium*. Compare *Survival.*

Spirit Photography
The photographing of supposed self-portraits of *discarnate entities* (called "extras") upon film or photographic plates. Compare *Photography, Paranormal.*

Spiritualism
Quasi-religious cult based upon the belief that *survival* of death is a reality, and upon the practice of communicating with deceased persons, usually via a *medium.*

Spontaneous Case
A discrete incident of *ostensible spontaneous psi.*

Stigmata
Term used to refer to the marks or hæmorrhages which appear spontaneously on the surface of the body in imitation of the wounds believed to have been received by Jesus Christ at the Crucifixion; sometimes observed on the bodies of certain devout individuals, and may also be induced by auto-suggestion or under

hypnosis. [Plural of the Greek *stigma*, "puncture, mark, spot"]

Subliminal

Term coined by Frederic Myers to refer to events occurring beneath the "threshold" of conscious awareness. [From the Latin *sub*, "below, under," + *limen (liminus)*, "threshold"]

Supernatural

A theological and folkloristic term for *paranormal*, generally avoided by parapsychologists because of its implication that *psi* is somehow "outside of" or "over and above" nature.

Superstition

A belief that a given action can bring good luck or bad luck when there are no rational or generally acceptable grounds for such a belief.

Survival

Continued existence of the consciousness of the individual person in some form and for at least some time after the destruction of their physical body; life-after-death; not to be considered synonymous with "immortality," which implies unending existence. See also *Reincarnation; Spirit Hypothesis.*

Synchronicity

Term coined by Carl Jung (with Wolfgang Pauli, 1955) to refer to the occurrence of acausal but meaningful *coincidences.* [From the Greek *synchronos*, derived from *synchronizein*, "to be contemporary with," derived from *syn-*, "with," + *chronos*, "time"]

Table-Tilting

A form of motor *automatism* in which several persons place their finger-tips on a table top, causing it to move and rap out messages by means of a code. Also called "table tipping" or "table turning." [Dale & White, 1977]

Tarot

A set of playing-cards first used in Italy in the fourteenth century, consisting of a series of 22 cards bearing figures (21 of them being numbered) and referred to as the "Major Arcanum," together with a set of 56 cards (in four suits) constituting the "Minor Arcanum," forming a pack of 78 cards.

Telekinesis

Older term for *"psychokinesis,"* coined by Alexander Aksakof (1895/1890), and still preferred in the former USSR; Soviet Union and Eastern Europe. [From the Greek *tele*, "far away," + *kinesis*, "a moving, disturbance," derived from *kinein*, "to set in motion"]

Telepathy

Term coined by Frederic Myers to refer to the *paranormal* acquisition of information concerning the thoughts, feelings or activity of another conscious being; the word has superseded earlier expressions such as "thought-transference." See also *General Extrasensory Perception*. [From the Greek *ele*, "far away," + *pathein*, "to have suffered, been affected by something"]

Latent Telepathy
An instance of telepathy in which there seems to be a time lag between the *agent's* attempt to transmit the *target*, and the *percipient's* awareness of that target.

Precognitive Telepathy
The paranormal acquisition of information concerning the future mental state of another conscious being.

Theosophy
In general, any school of thought claiming to have special insight into the nature of God; specifically, the religious and philosophical doctrines of the Theosophical Society, founded in 1875 in New York by Madame Helene Petrova Blavatsky based on Hindu and Buddhist notions, it taught the conscious development of *paranormal* abilities, and belief in reincarnation. [From the Greek *theos*, "God," + *sophia*, "wisdom"]

Thoughtography
See *Photography, Paranormal.*

Thought-Transference
See *Telepathy.*

Trance
A state of *dissociation* in which the individual is oblivious to their situation and surroundings, and in which various forms of *automatism* may be expressed; usually exhibited under *hypnotic, mediumistic* or *shamanistic* conditions. [From the

Old French *transe,* "passage," ultimately derived from the Latin *transire,* "to go across"]

Trance Personality

See *Communicator; Control.*

Transliminality

Term introduced by Michael A. Thalbourne (1991a), meaning literally "the tendency to cross the threshold into awareness." Persons exhibiting a high degree of transliminality are more likely to believe in, and claim experience of, *paranormal* phenomena, as well as to report more *magical ideation,* a more creative personality, more *mystical experience,* greater religiosity and more fantasy-proneness, as well as a history of experience resembling clinical depression and mania. Therefore, transliminality is defined as "susceptibility to, and awareness of, large volumes of imagery, ideation and emotion — these phenomena being stimulated by *subliminal, supraliminal* and/or external inputs." [From the Latin *trans,* "across, beyond," + *limen (liminis),* "threshold"]

Unorthodox Healing

See *Healing, Psychic.*

Veridical

Truthful; corresponding to, or conveying fact. Compare *Falsidical.* [From the Latin *veridicus,* derived from *verum,* "truth" + *dicere,* "to say"]

Voice Phenomena

See *Electronic Voice Phenomena.*

Writing, Automatic
See *Automatic Writing.*

Xenoglossy
Term coined by Charles Richet (1905) to denote the act of speaking in a language ostensibly unknown to the speaker. To be distinguished from glossolalia. [From the Greek *xenos*, "foreign, alien," + *glossa*, "language"]

Zener Cards
The original name given to the *ESP cards*; named after the perceptual psychologist Karl Zener, a colleague of Rhine's, who apparently suggested the symbols to be used on the cards (circle, cross, square, star, and wavy lines).

References

Aksakof, A. N. (1895). *Animisme et spiritisme.* Paris: P. G. Leymarie. (Original work published in 1890 in German in Leipzig.)

Ashby, R. H (1972). *Glossary of terms. The guidebook for the study of psychical research and parapsychology* (pp. 144-157). London: Rider.

Batcheldor, K. J. (1984). Contributions to the theory of PK induction from sitter-group work. *Journal of the American Society for Psychical Research, 78,* 105-122.

Beloff, J., & Bate, D. (1970). Research Report for the year 1968-69, University of Edinburgh Parapsychology Unit. *Journal of the Society for Psychical Research, 45,* 297-301.

Braud, W. G. (1978). Allobiofeedback: Immediate feedback for a psychokinetic influence upon another person's physiology. In W. G. Roll (Ed.), *Research in parapsychology, 1977* (pp. 123-134). Metuchen, New Jersey: Scarecrow Press.

Buchanan, J. R. (1893). *Manual of psychometry.* Boston: F. H. Hodges.

Dale, L., & White, R. A. (1977). Glossary of terms found in the literature of psychical research and parapsychology. In B. B. Wolman et al. (Eds.) *Handbook of parapsychology* (pp. 921-936). New York: van Nostrand Reinhold.

Dessoir, M. (1889). Die Parapsychologie, *Sphinx, 7,* 341-344.

Fukurai,T. (1931). *Clairvoyance and thoughtography.* London: Rider.

Hastings, A. (1990). Psi and the phenomena of channeling. In L. A. Henkel & J. Palmer, (Eds.), *Research in parapsychology 1989* (pp. 99-123). Metuchen, NJ: Scarecrow Press.

Jung, C. G., & Pauli, W. (1955). *The interpretation of nature and the psyche.* Princeton, NJ: Princeton University Press.

Myers, F. W. H. (1903). *Human personality and its survival of bodily death.* New York: Longmans, Green.

Nash, C. B. (1978). Appendix II. In *Science of psi* (pp. 237-249). Springfield, IL: Charles C Thomas.

Palmer, J. (1986) Terminological poverty in parapsychology: Two examples. In D. H. Weiner &. D. I. Radin (Eds.), *Research in parapsychology 1985* (pp.138-141) Metuchen, NJ: Scarecrow Press. [Abstract]

Richet, C. (1905). Xénoglossie: L'ecriture automatique en langues étrangères. *Proceedings of the Society for Psychical Research, 19,* 162-194.

Schmeidler, G. R. (1943). Predicting good and bad scores in a clairvoyance experiment: A preliminary report. *Journal of the American Society for Psychical Research, 37,* 103-110.

Targ, R. (1983). Proposed application of associational remote viewing to oil and natural resource recovery In W. G. Roll, J. Beloff, & R. A. White (Eds). *Research in parapsychology 1982* (pp. 264-266). Metuchen, NJ: Scarecrow Press. [Abstract]

Targ, R., & Puthoff, H. (1974). Information transmission under conditions of sensory shielding. *Nature, 251,* 602-607.

Thalbourne, M. A. (1991a). The psychology of mystical experience. *Exceptional Human Experience, 9,* 168-186.

Thalbourne, M. A. (1991b). The psychology of mystical experience. *Exceptional Human Experience, 9,* 269. [Abstract]

Vilenskaya, L. (1983). Two views of one book. *Psi Research, June,* 106-108.

White, R. A. (1994). Exceptional human experiences: The generic connection. *ASPR Newsletter, 18*(3), 1-6.

Wilson, S. C., & Barber, T. X. (1983). The fantasy-prone personality: Implications for understanding imagery, hypnosis, and parapsychological phenomena. In A. A. Sheikh (Ed.), *Imagery: Cur-*

rent theory, research, and application (pp. 340-387). New York: Wiley.

Zusne, L., & Jones, W. H. (1982). *Anomalistic psychology: A study of extraordinary phenomena of behavior and experience.* Hillsdale, NJ: Lawrence Erlbaum Associates.

❖ Notes ❖

❖ **Notes** ❖

❖ Notes ❖

❖ **Notes** ❖

❖ Notes ❖